China Briefing

The Practical Application of China Business

For further volumes:
http://www.springer.com/series/8839
http://www.asiabriefingmedia.com

Dezan Shira & Associates is a specialist foreign direct investment practice, providing business advisory, tax, accounting, payroll and due diligence services to multinationals investing in China, Hong Kong, India and Vietnam. Established in 1992, the firm is aleading regional practice in Asia with seventeen offices in four jurisdictions, employing over 170 business advisory and tax professionals.

We also provide useful business information through our media and publishing house, Asia Briefing.

Chris Devonshire-Ellis · Andy Scott ·
Sam Woollard
Editors

Setting Up Wholly Foreign Owned Enterprises in China

Third Edition

Springer DEZAN SHIRA & ASSOCIATES

Editors
Chris Devonshire-Ellis
Andy Scott
Sam Woollard
Dezan Shira & Associates
Asia Briefing Ltd.
Unit 1618, 16/F, Miramar Tower
132 Nathan Road
Tsim Sha Tsui, Kowloon
Hong Kong, People's Republic of China
e-mail: editor@asiabriefingmedia.com

ISBN 978-3-642-15539-0 e-ISBN 978-3-642-15540-6

DOI 10.1007/978-3-642-15540-6

Springer Heidelberg Dordrecht London New York

Library of Congress Control Number: 2010938322

Published by Springer-Verlag Berlin Heidelberg

Cover design: eStudio Calamar, Berlin/Figueres

Printed on acid-free paper

Springer is part of Springer Science+Business Media (www.springer.com)

About China Briefing's China Business Guides

Thank you for buying this book. China Briefing's publications are designed to fill a niche in the provision of information about business law and tax in China. When we decided, several years ago, to commence this series, we did so in the knowledge that much that was available about China was either expensive, or completely contradictory. Plus much of it did not really adequately address the real issues faced by businessmen—the practical knowledge that must be part of any business dealings in developing countries. This guide is designed to change that perspective and provide detailed information and the regulatory background to business in China—but with a firm eye also on the details of making money and remaining in compliance.

Accordingly, we have made this guide informative, easy to read and inexpensive. To do so we have engaged not a team of journalists or academics—but the services of a respected professional services firm to assist us. The articles and materials within have been researched and written by China-based Chinese and international lawyers, accountants and auditors, familiar with the issues that foreign invested enterprises face in China—as they service them in China as clients. These professionals have come from the nationally established practice, Dezan Shira & Associates, and we are grateful for their support. Without them this book would not have been possible, and we wholeheartedly recommend their services should you require sensible and pragmatic advice as contained within this book.

At China Briefing, our motto is "The practical application of China business" and we hope that within this volume and our other publications you feel we have achieved this, and helped point you in the right direction when it comes to understanding and researching this vast and complicated business environment.

Asia Briefing Publications
Hong Kong

Contents

Devising Your China Investment Strategy

1 Pre-investment Considerations

If you are contemplating setting up a business in China, you will need to consider what structure to use. But before deciding on the structure, you need to be sure of your *strategy—strategy must lead structure*. You must first consider *why* you want to make an investment in China, and find out just *what* you should be doing, before determining just *how* to do it.

Beware, especially, of the tendency to consider only a Joint Venture (JV) because it sounds warm and friendly—there are some situations when this is the right way to go, but increasingly, many foreign investors want to go it alone.

In this initial chapter, then, we will look at how you can decide what structure to choose; explain the structures that are available; introduce the core topic of this book, the Wholly Foreign-Owned Enterprise (WFOE); and lay out the key issues you will need to consider when you come to set up the business. In subsequent chapters we will discuss these issues and the establishment process in much more detail.

Why Do You Want to Come to China?

The five most common motivations for a new, or increased, China investment, identified by a contributor in one of our regional guidebooks, are:

- *customer pull*—key customer(s) want you to put more resources into China to better serve their needs, and you may need to do so in order to retain their business
- *attractive market*—there is an identified, *incremental* market opportunity for your products/services in China

C. Devonshire-Ellis et al. (eds.), *Setting Up Wholly Foreign Owned Enterprises in China*, China Briefing, DOI: 10.1007/978-3-642-15540-6_1,

- *competitive threat*—global competitors have a position here which could give them an advantage in cost or proximity to your customer base, and/or local Chinese competitors are starting to penetrate your home market
- *operational efficiencies/cost savings*—moving to China will improve your manufacturing and/or supply chain costs due to proximity to customers/suppliers, lower labour rates, etc.
- *stakeholder push*—there is tangible pressure from your company ownership (board, CEO, stockholders/Wall Street) to become active in China.

There may be several motivations in play of course, but almost every China investment boils down to one or more of these. Understanding which applies in your case will help you decide what the correct structure should be.

Equally, when choosing an appropriate investment vehicle, many factors must be considered, as these will lead to different legal and tax considerations. You will need to address questions such as:

- do you require an entity in mainland China or is a Hong Kong incorporation sufficient to reach your aims?
- do you need to invoice locally for services or products?
- are you getting a feel for the market or have you decided to commit to a larger scale operation?
- are you planning to set up a production-oriented entity (both for goods or services) or do you need only a representation in the country to carry out market research or liaison activities?
- will you be involved in trading, manufacturing, services or a combination of these?
- is the sector you are investing in fully open to foreign participation or do you still require a local partner?
- would you need to conduct the business alone, or would you require a Chinese company chipping in with assets or distribution networks?
- could the foreign enterprise itself carry out the business directly or through the medium of a separate, sometimes unrelated, entity in China?
- where should you be?—you will need to consider issues such as proximity to any China suppliers and raw materials; proximity to any Chinese customers; proximity to ports and other related infrastructure; costs of land and staff; and available incentives.

2 Options Concerning Foreign Investment Vehicles

There are several forms of enterprises from which you can choose. These include representative offices (RO), WFOE, foreign-invested commercial enterprises (FICE), and JVs. The table shows the main differing characteristics of these four structures.

Abbreviation	Type of structure	Legal status	Common purpose(s)	Pros	Cons
Choosing your China structure					
RO	Representative office	No legal personality	Market research, planning longer-term ventures, liaison with home country companies	Inexpensive to set up Allows exploration of the market and liaison activity	Cannot invoice locally in RMB Must recruit staff from local agency
WFOE	Wholly foreign-owned enterprise	Limited liability legal personality	Most manufacturing businesses (for China sales or export), some service businesses	100% ownership and control More flexible business scope Security of technology/IP Development of own infrastructure Insertion of existing company culture Allowed to convert RMB into foreign currency for profit repatriation	Need to fund registered capital requirement Development of China sales operations on your own

(continued)

(continued)

Abbreviation	Type of structure	Legal status	Common purpose(s)	Pros	Cons
FICE	Foreign-invested commercial enterprise	Limited liability legal personality	WFOE or JV mainly used for trading, distribution, and retail	As for normal WFOEs Specialised structure for trading, retailing and distribution	As for normal WFOEs New structure, implementation/registration process still bedding down
JV	Joint venture	Limited liability legal personality (in most cases)	When restrictions require local partner, or when they can offer e.g. scales and distributions channels	Use of existing facilities and workforce Use of existing sales/distribution channels Eager to secure long-term export sales	Management can be awkward Inheriting staff liabilities Over inflation of assets or sales in planning Technology transfer/IP/management risks Split profits

For the purposes of this book, we will assume that you have considered these options and decided that a WFOE—or a FICE (please note that FICE can be either in the form of a WFOE or a JV, the set up procedures for which are evidently different. FICE in this book refers to FICE in the form of a WFOE), which is a specialised kind of FIE—is your best bet. For more on ROs and JVs, see the other relevant books in this series.

What is a WFOE and Why Should You Choose It?

The Chinese government's initial aim in creating this form of company in 1986 was to encourage export-oriented manufacturing activities and to introduce advanced technology. They have steadily increased the scope of business allowed to such companies, and after joining the WTO, WFOEs were allowed in consulting and management services, software, development and trading. Further sectors will be progressively opened up in due course.

Their popularity has been steadily increasing. By 2009, WFOEs accounted for 76.3 percent of total international investment, and 77.4 percent for the first half of 2010, compared to 27% in 1995.

A WFOE is a company wholly owned by foreign investors. Note that in general international terminology, if there are several parties jointly investing in a company, this is commonly defined as a JV. However, according to Chinese law, when foreign parties are jointly investing in China, without any local partner, the company will always be regarded as a WFOE.

In legal terms, WFOEs are limited liability companies. The liability of the shareholders is limited to the assets they brought to the business.

Customisation of Your WFOE—Every WFOE is not the Same

It is worth noting that recently a "cookie-cutter" approach to structuring such entities has become increasingly prevalent. However, in the rush to get into the China market, many consultants, investors and other so-called "experts" have been advising, or have been advised, in a poor and simplistic manner. Equally, international businessmen have still shown themselves to be occasionally rather naïve when it comes to dealing with business operations in China.

- *Rule #1*—do not throw the rulebook away. Whatever made you have a successful business overseas, do not abandon it just because this is China. Be diligent, and be smart
- *Rule #2*—setting up a business in China requires China tax and China legal knowledge. Not one or the other, but both. You need to have professional advice in both these disciplines to get the most out of your business—before you start to invest
- *Rule #3*—cheap advice is dangerous. Everyone is an expert on China these days. Cheap advice is just that—cheap. Do your research. Professional firms are there

for a reason—depth of knowledge and understanding of China business and operational quirks and idiosyncrasies. Investing in China requires a great deal of attention to detail. Your WFOE needs customising to get the most out of it.

What to Think About When Creating Your WFOE

Again, remember, *strategy must lead structure*. It is important to choose to create a WFOE for the right reasons, as we discussed earlier. But it is equally important to choose the right structure for the WFOE itself, too, for *operational business reasons*, not because the legal rules might imply a particular direction.

We will go through these issues in much greater detail in the next chapter, but in the meantime here is a checklist of the issues you will need to consider:

- what will your business scope be?—foreign-invested enterprises, and indeed all domestic companies, have to operate within their business scope—this is more critical than in most western countries
- is your business in an "encouraged", "permitted", "restricted", or "prohibited" industry for foreign investment?—this will determine whether or not you can in fact create a WFOE, and whether it will lead to certain incentives
- what are the texts of your "Articles of Association"?—these will lead you to consider issues like board structure, profits repatriation, trade unions, M&A, and liquidation
- what should be your registered capital and total investment (cash, "in kind" loan)?—this is a *very important issue*, and you will need to focus on it from an *operational*, not regulatory, point of view—do not be swayed by legal minimums, which may be too low to actually run the business! Your capital needs will be driven by your business model, not the legal minimum guidelines
- if you are manufacturing, what proportion of your production is for export, and what for domestic sales?—again, a critical issue with major tax and operational implications—we explain further in subsequent chapters
- what taxes will you need to pay?—these are likely to include business tax, corporate income tax (with major changes having taken place in 2007), VAT, withholding tax, individual income tax, and customs duty—again, we will explain these in more detail
- where should your company be located?—this will depend on your specific sectoral needs, but you may have several options around the country, possibly including several different development zones, with differing characteristics and available incentives.

General Establishment Procedures

Different authorities will be involved at different steps of the approval procedure for any foreign entity in China. Throughout the incorporation process you will become more and more familiar with departments like the Administration of Industry and Commerce (AIC), the Bureau of Foreign Trade and Economic Cooperation (BOFTEC), the state and local tax bureaus, Customs and so forth.

The establishment procedure involves central, provincial or local level authorities approvals depending on the sector involved, the amount of the total investment and the location. The Ministry of Commerce (MOFCOM) is the final approval authority for a JV or a WFOE, but it delegates part of its power to its local counterparts, the BOFTEC at provincial and municipality levels. Some specific industries may require additional licensing.

3 WFOE Regulatory Issues and Implementing Rules

The fundamental legal basis for WFOEs is the *Law of the People's Republic of China on Foreign-invested Enterprises* (the WFOE Law), which became effective on April 12, 1986 and was subsequently revised on October 31, 2000.

Also very relevant are the Implementing Rules of the WFOE Law, which became effective December 12, 1990 and were subsequently revised April 12, 2001. The full text is available on request from info@dezshira.com.

On occasion, these need to be read in conjunction with the Company Law, the most recent version being that which became effective January 1, 2006.

Article 218 of the Company Law states:

"The limited liability companies and joint stock companies invested with foreign investment shall be governed by this law. Where the laws for foreign investment enterprises have other provisions, such other provisions shall be applicable."

In other words:

- the WFOE Law prevails
- but if the WFOE Law is silent on an issue, the Company Law applies.

We reproduce the full text of the WFOE Law below, with some commentary in italics.

Law of the People's Republic of China on Foreign-Invested Enterprises (the WFOE Law)

(Adopted at the fourth Meeting of the Sixth National People's Congress on April 12, 1986, amended in accordance with the Decision on Modifying the Law of the People's Republic of China on Foreign-Invested Enterprises adopted at the 18th Meeting of the Standing Committee of the Ninth National People's Congress on October 31, 2000)

Article 1. With a view to expanding economic cooperation and technical exchange with foreign countries and promoting the development of China's national economy, the People's Republic of China permits foreign enterprises, other foreign economic organisations and individuals (hereinafter referred to as "foreign investors") to establish foreign-invested enterprises in China and protects the legitimate rights and interests of such enterprises.

Article 2. As mentioned in this Law, "foreign-invested enterprises" refers to those enterprises established in China by foreign investors, exclusively with their own capital, in accordance with relevant Chinese laws. The term does not include branches established in China by foreign enterprises and other foreign economic organisations.

In other words, WFOEs only. ROs and JVs are governed by different laws.

Article 3. Foreign-invested enterprises shall be established in such a manner as to help the development of China's national economy. The state encourages the establishment of foreign-invested enterprises that export their products or have advanced technologies.

The Chinese policy objective is to support exports and advanced technology.

Provisions shall be made by the State Council regarding the lines of business which the state forbids foreign-invested enterprises to engage in or on which it places certain restrictions.

Namely, the "Catalogue of the Guidance for the Foreign Investment Industries," see below.

Article 4. The investments of a foreign investor in China, the profits it earns and its other lawful rights and interests are protected by Chinese law.

Foreign-invested enterprises must abide by Chinese laws and regulations and must not engage in any activities detrimental to China's public interest.

Article 5. The state shall not nationalise or requisition any foreign-invested enterprise. Under special circumstances, when public interest requires, foreign-invested enterprises may be requisitioned by legal procedures and appropriate compensation shall be made.

Article 6. The application to establish a foreign-invested enterprise shall be submitted for examination and approval to the department under the State Council in charge of foreign trade and economic cooperation, or to any other agency authorised by the State Council. The authorities in charge of examination and approval shall, within 90 days from the date it receives such application, decide whether or not to grant approval.

However, under certain very occasional circumstances, this may be prolonged for further investigation or clarification should the approvals authority deem this necessary.

Article 7. After an application for the establishment of a foreign-invested enterprise has been approved, the foreign investor shall, within 30 days from the date of receiving a certificate of approval, apply to the industry and commerce administration authority for registration and obtain a business license. The date of issuance of the business license shall be the date of the establishment of the enterprise.

Article 8. An enterprise with foreign capital that meets the conditions for being considered a legal person under Chinese law shall acquire the status of a Chinese legal person, in accordance with the law.

Article 9. A foreign-invested enterprise shall make investments in China within the period approved by the authorities in charge of examination and approval. If it fails to do so, the industry and commerce administration authority may cancel its business license.

In other words, there are time limits for bringing in your registered capital.

The industry and commerce administration authority shall inspect and supervise the investment situation of a foreign-invested enterprise.

Article 10. In the event of a split, merger or other major change, a foreign-invested enterprise shall report to and seek approval from the authorities in charge of examination and approval, and register the change with the industry and commerce administration authority.

Article 11. Foreign-invested enterprises shall conduct their operations and management in accordance with the approved articles of association, and shall be free from any interference.

Which is why it is so important to get the articles right first time!

Article 12. When employing Chinese workers and staff, a foreign-invested enterprise shall conclude contracts with them according to law, in which matters concerning employment, dismissal, remuneration, welfare benefits, labor protection and labor insurance shall be clearly prescribed.

Article 13. Workers and staff of a foreign-invested enterprise may organise trade unions in accordance with the law so as to conduct trade union activities and protect their lawful rights and interests.

The enterprises shall provide the necessary conditions for the activities of the trade unions in their respective enterprises.

There is currently some pressure from Chinese trade unions to make it obligatory for foreign-invested enterprises to form trade unions.

Article 14. A foreign-invested enterprise must set up account books in China, conduct independent accounting, submit the financial reports and statements as required and accept supervision by the financial and tax authorities.

If a foreign-invested enterprise refuses to keep account books in China, the financial and tax authorities may impose a fine on it, and the industry and commerce administration authority may order it to suspend operations or may revoke its business license.

Article 15. Within the approved scope of the operations, foreign-invested enterprises may, according to the principles of fairness and reason, purchase raw and semi-processed materials, fuels and other materials they need either in China or from the world market.

Article 16. Foreign-invested enterprises shall apply to insurance companies in China for such kinds of insurance coverage as are needed.

Article 17. Foreign-invested enterprises shall pay taxes in accordance with relevant state provisions for tax payment, and may enjoy preferential treatment for reduction of or exemption from taxes.

A foreign-invested enterprise that reinvests in China its profits after paying the income tax, may, in accordance with relevant state provisions, apply for refund of a part of the income tax already paid on the reinvested amount.

Article 18. Foreign-invested enterprises shall handle their foreign exchange transactions in accordance with the state provisions for foreign exchange control.

Foreign-invested enterprises shall open an account with the Bank of China or with a bank designated by the state agency exercising foreign exchange control.

Article 19. Foreign investors may remit abroad profits that are lawfully earned from a foreign-invested enterprise, as well as other lawful earnings and any funds remaining after the enterprise is liquidated.

Wages, salaries and other legitimate income earned by foreign employees in a foreign-invested enterprise may be remitted abroad after the payment of individual income tax in accordance with the law.

Article 20. With respect to the term of operations of a foreign-invested enterprise, the foreign investor shall report to and secure approval from the authorities in charge of examination and approval. For an extension of the term of operations, an application shall be submitted to the said authorities 180 days before the expiration of the period. The authorities in charge of examination and approval shall, within 30 days from the date such application is received, decide whether or not to grant the extension.

Article 21. When terminating its operations, a foreign-invested enterprise shall promptly issue a public notice and proceed with liquidation in accordance with legal procedure.

Pending the completion of liquidation, a foreign investor may not dispose of the assets of the enterprise except for the purpose of liquidation.

Article 22. At the termination of operations, the foreign-invested enterprise shall nullify its registration with the industry and commerce administration authority and hand in its business license for cancellation.

Article 23. The department under the State Council which is in charge of foreign economic relations and trade shall, in accordance with this Law, formulate rules for its implementation, which shall go into effect after being submitted to and approved by the State Council.

Article 24. This Law shall go into effect on the day of its promulgation.

4 Encouraged Industry Applications

You will also need to determine the official status of your industry sector, and whether or not you can in fact create a WFOE, or if you need some form of Chinese involvement as a JV partner.

To do so, you should refer to the so-called Catalogues – there are two different documents, the first is the Catalogue for the Guidance of Foreign Investment

Industries, which applies to the whole of China; the second is the Catalogue of Priority Industries for Foreign Investment in the Central-Western Region.

The Catalogue for the Guidance of Foreign Investment was published by the National Development and Reform Commission (NDRC) and the Ministry of Commerce. It categorizes different industries in China as "encouraged," "permitted," "restricted," and "prohibited" to foreign investment. These categories are defined as follows:

- "permitted"—any industry not listed in another category is "permitted"
- "encouraged"—these include sectors that promote the development of agriculture, involve high technology, upgrade product quality, promote environmental protection, promote exports and which will help in the development of the poorer and less-developed interior regions—these sectors get some special incentives
- "restricted"—these industries include those that are technologically backward, environmentally unfriendly or industries that are being opened up to foreign investment on a pilot basis
- "prohibited"—these industries are those that use technology unique to China or, not surprisingly, which harm the national interest, are damaging to the environment or human health, jeopardise security or are politically sensitive.

Certain industries under both the "encouraged" and "restricted" categories are only permitted for Sino-foreign joint venture enterprises or other entities with a limited percentage of foreign investment. The latest version of the catalogue was published in 2007. An English version of the 2007 edition can be obtained on request from info@dezshira.com. On April 1, 2011, the Legislative Affairs of the State Council published the draft 2011 Catalogue for the Guidance of Foreign Investment Industries for public comments. The comment period ended on April 30, 2011 and the draft is expected to be adopted in the next quarter.

The draft 2011 Foreign Investment Catalogue added more environmentally-friendly and high-end projects to the "encouraged" category, including new materials deemed to be environmentally-friendly, automotive parts and components that result in energy savings, environmentally-friendly battery manufacturing technology, the construction of water recycling facilities, and investment in charging facilities for electric vehicles. Other industry sectors and products/services, including aviation, aerospace, light motorcycles, advanced generation equipment for Internet and network systems, advanced semiconductor development, and exploration and exploitation of unconventional natural gas resources, were also included in the "encouraged" category.

The draft Catalogue also reflects China's desire to further restrict projects that require heavy energy consumption or cause elevated levels of pollution, as well as to impose stricter controls on its housing bubbles by prohibiting foreign investment in the construction and operation of villas.

The latest version of the Catalogue of Priority Industries for Foreign Investment in the Central-Western Region was published in 2008 and entered into force on

January 1, 2009, replacing the 2004 version of the catalogue as well as the 2006 Catalogue of Priority Industries for Foreign Investment in Liaoning Province. The catalogue contains a total of 411 priority industries in 21 provinces and autonomous regions in the central and western regions, i.e., Shanxi, Jilin, Heilongjiang, Anhui, Jiangsu, Henan, Hubei, Hunan, Chongqing, Sichuan, Guizhou, Yunnan, Tibet, Shaanxi, Gansu, Qinghai, Ningxia, Xinjiang, Inner Mongolia, Guangxi and Liaoning. Unlike the Catalogue for the Guidance of Foreign Investment Industries, this catalogue contains only priority industries, and all projects listed in the catalogue enjoy preferential policies applied towards foreign investment in the "encouraged" sectors, including the ability to obtain custom duty exemption on imported equipment.

- Currently, the lion's share of FDI remains in manufacturing, but significant amounts are starting to drift into services and the tertiary sector, and indeed into the primary sector, as more areas are opened up and the economy becomes more sophisticated.

Applying for "Encouraged" Status

As with all business applications, these first need to go to the Ministry of Commerce or its regional office for the Approval Certificate, then to the regional office again for the business licence. For encouraged status applications, these now need to be approved by the National Development and Reform Commission.

It is worth noting that—as in many cases in China—officials do appear to apply some administrative discretion to the definitions within these categories. For example, we have been able to negotiate cases where a manufacturer wished to manufacture product A, but this was not in an "encouraged" industry. However, a by-product of their process, product B, was in an "encouraged" industry. It proved possible to frame their business scope around product B, not product A and therefore obtain encouraged industry status.

NDRC issued a notice FGWZ [2006] No. 316 on February 22, 2006, to provide more details on certification procedures for encouraged projects, define more clearly who the responsible approving authorities are, and warn against abuses.

Major points of the notice are as follows:

- for a foreign invested project with total investment over US$30 million, the project approval paper should be issued by NDRC
- for projects under US$30 million, the project approval papers should be issued by a Provincial Development and Reform Commission
- no entities other than NDRC or its provincial agencies have authority to issue the approval paper

The procedures apply both to initial approval of Sino-foreign Equity JVs (EJVs), Sino-foreign cooperative JVs (CJVs) and wholly foreign-owned enterprises (WFOEs), and increases in total investments of existing EJVs, CJVs and WFOEs. Further filings for tax exemption on imported goods need to be made with the customs and tax bureaus.

The notice also emphasises that a project with total investment in excess of US$30 million cannot be "compartmentalized" to avoid the scrutiny of the NDRC. Similarly FIEs are warned that they must not understate the amount of total investment and apply for an increase after a project and corresponding exemption are approved. Applicants and local approving agencies are also warned against unwarranted "stretching" of the meaning of exempt criteria. NDRC says it would strengthen review of approvals granted in respect of projects below US$30m to identify irregularities. Violations may lead not only to withdrawal of exemption, but also disruption of importation and hence serious financial damages to those involved.

If a WFOE applies to be evaluated as "encouraged sector" after its establishment, such as in the case with an alteration or addition to its scope of business, or in the event this had previously been overlooked, the company would need to supply the following documents to the authorities:

- application form
- copy of Business License
- Feasibility Study Report
- Certificate of Approval
- list of imported machinery and equipment with description of number, unit price, total price etc.

If the application involves an increase of capital, an audit report should also be submitted to the original approval authority.

5 Conclusion

It is important to be aware if your intended activities in China fall into the "encouraged" sector. If so, and you and your advisors are aware of this, your company may apply for significant benefits in the reduction of tax, and even profits tax holidays, depending upon the specific case. However, if you are not aware of these benefits and do not make a specific application to apply for them, your business stands to lose out significantly in terms of saved revenues.

Structuring Your WFOE

So you have decided to set up a WFOE. Now what? You need to work on the structure. In this chapter we will look at the issues surrounding the setting up of assembly and manufacturing WFOEs, trading/retail WFOEs (Foreign Invested Commercial Enterprises, FICEs), and service WFOEs.

Establishing entities of these kinds in China is a relatively straightforward procedure, if you know what you are doing. As we have already noted, it is certainly *not* an off the shelf administrative application and the completion of a few sheets of paper. You need to put careful thought into the application, and there are serious *operational* issues lurking behind what appear to be simply regulatory questions.

1 Structuring Manufacturing WFOES

There are several major, inter-related issues to address if you intend to set up a manufacturing WFOE in China:

- *business scope*—what should yours be?
- *registered capital requirements*—these may vary depending on the industry and the location. It is also *absolutely critical* that you do not simply put in the minimum because the regulations say you can—you may find the business is under-capitalised if you do so. This is an *operational* judgment for you, not the bureaucrats.
- *are you manufacturing 100% for export, or part for export, part for domestic sales?* Where are your clients located? Do they require an official local invoice? Would they require you to sell your goods to Hong Kong or other off-shore jurisdictions?—this has a fundamental impact on how you structure the business!

C. Devonshire-Ellis et al. (eds.), *Setting Up Wholly Foreign Owned Enterprises in China*, China Briefing, DOI: 10.1007/978-3-642-15540-6_2,

- *Articles of Association*—these need detailed work by you to ensure you cover all the bases. You are setting up a company with a 20–30 year life span, and you need to be sure you know what you are getting into.
- *tax holidays*—assembly and manufacturing WFOEs may still be eligible for *taxholidays* against Corporate Income Tax (depending on their date of inauguration), but service WFOEs and FICEs are not—make sure you choose the right structure.

We will now explore these in more detail.

Business Scope

Having set up a limited company does not necessarily mean you can engage in any kind of business activity, as is the case in some Western countries. WFOEs can only operate within the business scope approved by the authorities. Other activities are subject to further approval. So it is vital to determine what you want to do right from the start.

Lazy, or deliberately disingenuous, business scopes, such as only using the phrase "production of (product)", will not necessarily qualify a FIE as a production company. We have encountered numerous problems of this nature, all requiring a scope of business change on the licence before the tax bureau is satisfied. You need to ensure your business scope is accurate. Attempts to fool the tax bureau into thinking you are one thing, while in fact you are another—even if you can get it past the approvals process—inevitably end in failure. Play the game and say what it is you are really doing.

Registered Capital Requirements: Avoiding Under-Capitalisation Miseries

One of the most common, and most serious, problems with WFOE applications, especially for small businesses, is the issue over registered capital. This is a much misunderstood area. Confusion exists, and many ill-advised investments are made due to misinterpretation of the local government's term "minimum registered capital". It is not supposed to be a ruling on how much you need to invest. Registered capital is the initial investment in the company that is immediately used in its operation – part of the "working capital" if you like. Get this wrong and it is financially painful to change it.

The official requirements vary from industry to industry, and also on a regional basis. A WFOE wanting to establish in Beijing may face different capital requirements than one in Tianjin, Shanghai or Dongguan. Also, some regions have their own regional incentive policies encouraging foreign investment and require lower registered capital. So, if you can be flexible on location, shop around and compare regional differences. With much of China's eastern and southern coastal areas possessing sound import–export infrastructure, it may be more efficient to place the factory in one of the second-tier cities—capital requirements and operating costs vary quite considerably.

Additionally, there is often conflict here between the local government—keen on securing another foreign investor in order to meet its targets—and other government departments, responsible for monitoring and managing China business issues, especially the tax bureau and customs.

It is important to note that tax collection is administered centrally, while the approvals process is at a local level. This means conflicts can and do arise between what the local government says in order to attract your investment, and what the tax bureau then says in dealing with any lack of compliance. And by then it is too late—you are already committed—and you have no choice other than to go through additional pain and hassle to get things put right, usually involving more investment.

In fact, some local government officials are downright reckless when using "minimum registered capital requirements" as a sales pitch. The amounts they may state may not be in compliance with the actual needs of businesses or other government department requirements—the classic obfuscation that so often blurs the thinking and otherwise competent planning by international investors. There are also many, many consultants out there who are also either blissfully unaware and ignorant of the real importance of registered capital and how to cater for it properly, or downright calculating, knowing that under-capitalisation can drive additional business their way from the unfortunate investor if they play the scenario correctly.

So why are there capital requirements?

- the authorities use capital as an entry barrier to ensure FIEs are of the relevant quality and financial strength
- in addition, such rules protect suppliers and others involved in the company's business from any incurring liability.

Wherever you site your WFOE, however, basic investment criteria remain the same, the government will look at the general viability of the project and a reasonable cash requirement for a particular type of investment. Injections of cash and plant only take place after the WFOE licence is approved, so it is a no-risk investment in terms of money up-front.

Registered capital and total investment figures are both required to be specified in the Feasibility Study Report and the WFOE's Articles of Association before the approval certificate is issued. Unlike registered capital, which has to be fully paid into the WFOE's Chinese bank account before starting business operations, the total investment quota is the total amount of funds planned to be contributed to the project over its lifespan and it does not necessarily have to be fully deposited in thebank account

The *Provisional Rules on the Ratio between Registered Capital and Total Investment of Sino-foreign Equity Joint Venture Enterprises* applies to the registered capital and total investment ratio of all foreign-invested enterprises, including WFOEs. The mandated ratio is expressed in the table below:

Total Investment (USD)	Registered Capital (Min.)
3 Million (inclusive) or below	7/10 of the Total Investment
3 Million (not inclusive) to 4.2 Million (not inclusive)	2.1 Million
4.2 Million (inclusive) to 10 Million (inclusive)	1/2 of the Total Investment
10 Million (not inclusive) to 12.5 Million (not inclusive)	5 Million
12.5 Million (inclusive) to 30 Million (inclusive)	2/5 of the Total Investment
30 Million (not inclusive) to 36 Million (not inclusive)	12 Million
36 Million (inclusive) or above	1/3 of the Total Investment

The difference between registered capital and total investment represents the debt of the investment and can be made up by loans from the investor or foreign banks. Pay attention to the relationship between registered capital and total investment in case you need to obtain further debt or other financing from your holding company or other financial institution. Keeping this window open will cost you nothing, but closing yourself off from further financing by equating registered capital and total investment may leave you handcuffed. The payment schedule of the WFOE registered capital also needs to be specified in the Articles of Association. The investor may choose to pay it as a lump sum or in installments

Registered Capital: How Much is Enough?

So how much do you have to pay? Under the Company Law, which came into force on January 1, 2006, absolute minimum capital requirements are:

- for multiple shareholder companies RMB30,000 (Article 26)
- for single shareholder companies RMB100,000 (Article 59).

However, in terms of foreign-invested companies, these figures are very misleading. Article 26 of the Law also states, "if any law or administrative regulation prescribes a relatively higher minimum amount of registered capital of a limited liability company, the provisions of that law or administrative regulation shall be followed."

And as we explain below, the government will look at project feasibility rather than minimum registered capital.

In addition, your registered capital is also your limited liability status. So the higher it is, the more credit worthy you are. But the real question for you is, what the Chinese authorities will consider as an adequate capitalisation for a specific project? This will be analysed case by case based on the Feasibility Study Report—and in the major FDI destinations they have done this many times, so they probably know what they are talking about (further inland, that may not always be the case).

However, remember, if the government specifies a minimum "X", and you think you need "Y", and "Y" is bigger, put in "Y"—or ensure you have "Y" from a combination of registered capital and debt financing.

The amount of registered capital needed in the business depends on a number of different factors, some regulatory and some operational:

- *location (regulatory)*—some regions in China apply different levels of capital requirements than others to reflect their lower or higher regional operational costs.
- *business scope (regulatory)*—for certain industries or services, the applicable registered capital amount can be quite high. This is sometimes used as a protectionist tool to discourage foreign investment, and/or to ensure only the right standard of international business can enter the market, thus guaranteeing the quality of the applicant—banking for example has a minimum of US$30 million. Please note that if some existing businesses wish to expand their current scope of business, it may be a requirement to increase the amount of registered capital.
- *Cashflow (operational)*—this is critical and often overlooked. Registered capital is also required to fund the business operations until it is in a position to fund itself. This should be catered for in the Feasibility Study Report. However, in the rush to attract new investments, and as a result of a lack of even basic economics, many government agents do not pay much attention to detail in this report. Often the happy foreign investor will naively assume he is got a great deal with a "minimum amount" being identified. However, the business can come to a shuddering halt if the registered capital amount is insufficient to support operational cash flow.

Correcting this is not just a simple matter of wiring additional funds to China. Procedures have to be followed since any money sent to make up an operational shortfall that does not follow the government's business cash injection protocol is assumed to be taxable income and can be subject to the 25 percent corporate income tax:

- application to increase the registered capital with the original approval authority
- application to the State Administration of Foreign Exchange to transfer funds into China
- bank to bank fund transfer.
- capital verification by local CPA firm
- re-issuing of business licence reflecting this—important as the registered capital amount is also the limited liability status of the business

The above steps take between 4 to 8 weeks to fulfill. If you have already run out of operational money, you by now have not paid staff for 2 months, your suppliers, and possibly your utilities. In effect, your business has been throttled before it even had a chance to breathe.

Registered Capital: The Mechanics

Registered capital can be contributed in cash or in kind, the latter normally being imported equipment or perhaps intellectual property rights (although in kind contributions cannot exceed 70 percent of the registered capital). Note that it can be time-consuming to inject equipment as a registered capital, rather than buying it using the registered capital cash. Locally obtained RMB cannot be injected as registered capital—it must be sent in from the overseas investor.

Reclaiming Registered Capital

After the registered capital is wired into the registered capital account in China, this amount cannot be wired out again freely. The money will be used as operational costs. Some advisors may tell you that you do not need actually to wire the money into China, or they can help you wire the registered capital out of China after the capital is verified. This is totally illegal—do not do this.

Operational Issues that Affect Your WFOE Structure

Different types of WFOE operations require different kinds of structuring. How to go about it depends on what you want to achieve.

Manufacturing, Processing and Assembly, 100 percent for Export

The Chinese love this type of operation and will reward you with some incentives and tax breaks. If you are sited in a Free Trade Zone or Export Processing Zone (see later in the book for more on the different types of development zones), you may not even have any import–export duties to worry about.

Basic tax breaks are against Corporate Income Tax, which is 25% nationally.

Certain sectors, such as agriculture and high-tech, can offer some tax deductions. If you export 100% of your production, then more incentives may kick in. For more on these issues, see the tax section and the section on development zones, and take professional advice!

You will need to consider the impact of VAT refunds on exports—we explain this in detail in chapter titled China's Business Taxes.

Manufacturing, Processing and Assembly, Part or All Domestic Sales

The domestic sales aspect fundamentally changes the tax structure of the WFOE, as it is then subject to import duties on any imported components and VAT at 17 percent on sales (import duties will vary depending on product, location and final customer). Under recent changes, WFOEs can now sell the majority, if not all, of their production domestically, thus tapping into the increasingly attractive local market. It is still wise, however, when structuring your WFOE to include a provision allowing you to sell your product on the domestic market "according to China's WTO agreements," thus permitting you to upgrade your domestic sales quota automatically without having to go through a constant process of updating your business licence whenever a change occurs. You still get the tax breaks, but would not qualify for rebates on CIT or other taxes as these only apply to WFOEs exporting 100 percent of production.

Other Issues to Consider

Sending Start-up Funds to China Before the WFOE Licence is Issued

It normally takes at least 4 months to complete a properly structured manufacturing WFOE application. However, some foreign investors are advised of tighter time frames, and advised to send the start-up funds to their local agent or local staff to cover the cost for the initial office fit-out, overhead or even equipment purchases. The problem is that these funds from the WFOE parent overseas cannot be recognised as part of your capital injection once the business license is issued, as the capital injection has to be transferred by the foreign investor from their overseas account to the nominated Capital Account directly, and *not* via any third party. Even if the money originated from overseas, as soon as it arrives in China it cannot be re-sent to the WFOE account as registered capital. In fact, it will be deemed taxable income.

It is far better to arrange this as an internal loan between the parent and the WFOE, and book it as a "rollover" amount not included as part of the WFOE registered capital requirements.

Alternatively, the foreign investor, after the WFOE name is registered at the State Administration for Industry and Commerce (SAIC) and even before the WFOE license is obtained, can open a temporary bank account for limited transactions covering construction costs and others which can count towards the WFOE registered capital contribution.

Different Location for Office and Factory?

We are sometimes asked whether a WFOE can register with a small office in a development zone with preferential policies, but build its factory elsewhere. The answer, not surprisingly, is no.

Firstly, a manufacturing WFOE is required to rent a factory space as their registered address. The local AIC will physically check the factory space before registering the WFOE. If this registered address is just a virtual address, you may not be able to pass the annual inspection because you are not really operating there. The authorities are becoming stricter on these sorts of issues, and we do not recommend that you attempt such ploys.

Trading Via WFOEs

If you are a manufacturing business, you may still import and distribute products not manufactured in China under an amended manufacturing WFOE licence—provided the amount does not "in general" exceed 30–50 percent of the total revenues, depending on the region. This means that manufacturing WFOEs can still trade as mentioned above, as long as the trading portion remains the minority part of the business. This is worth considering as a structure if your business model requires both, for example if your clients may occasionally require additional spare parts (import and trading service) or other maintenance issues. Note that approval needs to be obtained for this, including tax bureau permission. Your books also need to be accurate, well-organised and will be subject to scrutiny by the tax bureau to ensure you are in compliance.

2 Foreign Invested Commercial Enterprises

As part of its WTO accession process, China ratified regulations that permit foreign companies to establish fully operational WFOE retail and trading companies that can buy and sell in China. These rules became effective from June 1, 2004.

What Does The Law Say?

The *Measures for the Administration of Foreign Investment in the Commercial Sector* liberalised China's distribution and retail sector. Foreign companies are now allowed to establish:

- majority Joint Venture trading companies
- WFOE trading companies.

In detail, the new regulations apply to the following five activities:

- Retailing—i.e. selling goods and related services to individual persons from a fixed location, as well as through TV, telephone, mail order, internet, and vending machines.

Note that all geographical restrictions for retailing enterprises have been removed, and foreign investors can establish retail stores anywhere in China.

- Wholesaling—i.e. selling goods and related services to companies and customers from the industry, trade or other organisations
- representative transactions on the basis of provisions (agent, broker)
- franchising
- import/export, distribution and retailing by existing manufacturing companies.

Limitations do, however, apply to some specific products. Namely, if a foreign investor in China has more than 30 retail stores that distribute products such as books, periodicals, and processed oils from different brands or suppliers, the foreign investor's share in the retail enterprise is limited to 49 percent. Retailing enterprises which do not distribute the limited products are not restricted on the number of stores in China.

The regulations for commercial franchises that came into effect on May 1, 2007 reflect generally the Chinese Government's willingness to adopt a more liberal regulatory system towards foreign enterprises operating in this field.

Set-up Requirements

Foreign investors will enjoy national treatment in setting up trading companies with minimum registered capital in accordance with the Company Law of China:

- for wholesale and retail enterprises (single shareholder), RMB100,000.

But remember what we said above about registered capital for manufacturing WFOEs—the same operational logic applies and you must ensure that the registered capital is sufficient for your initial cash flow, not simply to satisfy regulatory needs. Have you considered all your working capital needs? And issues such as placing a bond with customs for imports? Or how to apply for VAT rebates on export? If not, you can get into trouble very quickly indeed if your registered capital needs are insufficient.

Business duration is limited to 30 years for foreign trading companies set up in the developed coastal areas—companies established in the West of China are allowed business duration of 40 years. Foreign companies shall "possess a sound reputation and comply with Chinese law".

3 Structuring Service WFOES

These vary in terms of permissible activities—quite a few sectors remain closed for foreign investors. However, there are many service industry businesses operating in China as WFOEs, including architects, language training schools, recruitment agencies, and healthcare companies.

As early as in the 1997 version of the Catalogue for the Guidance of Foreign Investment Industries, for international consulting firms with a good track record,

WFOE's in the consulting field are permitted to be registered, as long as they focused on "consultation of international economy, technology & environmental protection". The 2007 version of the Catalogue continue to retain this, and the 2011 draft Catalogue further included logistics information consulting. The 2007 Catalogue also included modern logistics and service outsourcing in the "encouraged" category' while the draft 2011 Catalogue encourages venture investment enterprises and IPR services. However, applications for these licences are still heavily monitored and not easy to come by' requiring detailed and exhaustive registration procedures.

4 The Feasibility Study Report

While you are not held to the contents of the report, it is used by the National Statistics Bureau to assess FDI in China. It is also used to assess exactly how much thought and planning has gone into your business, and although is often somewhat disregarded as a vital component of the process these days, it is nonetheless a good discipline to go through. Be professional about it and get a well thought out feasibility report put together. They do follow a standard format and this is provided by the authorities to you as part of your application documentation. It usually only comprises ten points—however it does need translation into Chinese and you will need administrative assistance to complete this.

5 Articles of Association

Many foreign investors nowadays seem to regard WFOE applications as just that—an administrative procedure that can be left to local managers or development zone advisors to handle. Seduced by the "fast service, one stop shop" approach, and the desire to keep friendly relations with government, many foreign investors seem quite content to spend a minimum amount of time looking at the articles. This is a mistake. When establishing a company with a likely 20–30 year lifespan, you'd better know what it is you are agreeing to. Articles are the operating rules of the company and it is vital they are properly structured. If not, you can create problems later on, and even lose out on benefits almost from day one. You *must* devote serious management time to these.

Here we highlight some of the articles, what they mean, and what should be included. We have also included a sample set of Articles of Association so you can see the sort of text that is required.

Scope of Business Article

As mentioned earlier, this needs to be detailed, as well as honest. If it is too wide or not clear enough it can cause post-licensing problems with the tax bureau if you are applying for tax breaks and incentives as well, and additionally with customs. It is extremely unwise to try and manipulate a scope of business to try and get tax breaks into your business if your actual activities do not warrant this, and avoid consultants or even development zone officials who try to persuade you otherwise. It should be straight forward, clear, and open, while leaving scope for the future expansion of your operations by including as much as you can—within reason.

Production Scale Article

This can be useful in terms of expressing an exit strategy. If you link production and profitability scales to what you would consider unacceptable levels of business thus requiring liquidation, it makes it far easier to obtain approval for closure if this eventuality occurs. You should also link production and profitability scales to the Liquidation Articles later in the document.

Total Investment Article

As discussed above, there is a relationship between your registered capital and your total investment capital, and this needs to be worked out as it can affect debt financing and the ability to obtain parent company loans.

Board of Directors Article

Keep it small (indeed the regulations also allow for only one executive director board structure as well!) and allow for board meetings to be held externally from China or even by telephone conference. Emergency board meetings, being just that—an emergency—should be called at 24 h and not 1 month's notice!

General Manager Article

This is a legally responsible position so put it in the hands of someone you trust—ideally your expat manager in charge of production. Limit the term of office to an annual period to give you some leeway. GM's can be notoriously difficult to fire if under the long terms identified in the standard articles.

Profits Repatriation Article

Cannot find it in the basic draft? That is because it is not there. This needs to be built in—essentially giving your parent company the right to bill the WFOE for services for management expertise, royalties, licensing agreements, interest on loans, R&D cost allocations, sales and marketing cost allocations and so on. If you do not have these drafted in it becomes difficult to overlay the service contracts into the articles and obtain approval for this mechanism. It could save you a significant amount on your profits tax bill.

Merger and Acquisition

Again, not in basic drafts. So if you want to sell the business how can you value it? It is easier to identify a set of rules beforehand. Identify asset valuers, accountants and industry professionals who can value the business. Make their decision final and binding with a time limit for offers to be accepted or bettered, and a mechanism for payment and share transfer itself. You never know what will happen down the road and who can tell what China or your business will be like in 5 years?

Liquidation Article

As mentioned earlier, try and link this to the production and profitability scales. Typically they are rather woolly meaning interpretation can creep in—and the local Government, whose approval is required—may have different ideas as to what is and what is not a liquidation scenario. Tie this to unacceptable, defined production and profitability levels and it is easier to exit if you need to.

Trade Union Article

Your staff has the right to form a trade union if there are more than 25 personnel—including expatriates (who may also join the union); if members are less than 25, a basic-level trade union committee may be established. Make sure you work out how to control the budget and influence its expenditure.

If a union is formed, then the elected representative has the right to attend company management meetings, and the company must fund also the union, with 2 percent of all employees' salaries, each month (staff must also make a small contribution). It is not uncommon for these funds to be misused, and for the union representative to become a bit of a nuisance as well. Funds should be used for workers education, welfare and entertainment, and many of the factory basketball courts you see in China have been funded in this manner. Funds may also be used to provide legal support to employees with grievances against the company.

Management interference can be minimised by restricting the union representative access only to the portion of meetings during which staff and workers rights are to be discussed, while budgets for the use of union funds can also be agreed upon and implemented. We recall a case a few years ago when union funds were used to buy the representative air conditioning at his home and a car! So, some measures of control can be exercised via the articles of association as concerns the role of the labour union.

Maintaining Currency Consistencies in the Articles and Business License

When applying for your business license, it is important to pay attention to detail when completing the business licence application and cross-referencing this against the articles. For example, as does occur, sometimes the capital amount to be registered on their business license is shown in RMB, however, the Articles identifies this amount in Euros or US$.

Consequently, if the exchange rate fluctuates, the injection verified by the local CPA firm, required to prove the registered capital transfer was made, may no longer match the figures on the business license. The registered capital converted into RMB may be less than the promised capital amount. So, you, the investor, have to transfer more funds. You also have to complete another capital verification, which you need to arrange with a local CPA firm and pay for, all of which is an annoyance and wastes your money and time.

Sample Articles of Association

Here we provide a basic draft set of WFOE articles as commonly used in China. As we have discussed, these should be studied in great detail and redrafted in accordance with your specific situation. Once completed, these need to be translated into Chinese and form part of the application documentation. It is important that you seek professional advice from a competent firm in China when drafting these, as any amendments to them require specific additional government approval—the granting of amendments being not entirely in the investors own hands.

Chapter 1

General provisions

Article 1

In accordance with the *Foreign Enterprise Law of the People's Republic of China* and other applicable laws and regulations, the Articles of Association are hereby formulated.

Article 2

The Chinese name of the investor is:
The English name of the investor is:
Registered in:
Legal address:
Legal representative:

Article 3

The company shall be a limited liability company operated by a wholly foreign-owned limited company, with limited liability based on its registered capital.

Article 4

The company is approved to be set up and registered in (location) by (name of government authority). It has the status of a legal person and is subject to the jurisdiction and protection of the laws of the PRC. All its activities shall be governed by the laws of the PRC and other pertinent rules and regulations.

Chapter 2

Purpose and scope of business

Article 5

Adhering to the principle of strengthening economic cooperation and technical interchange, the purpose of the company is to (fill in appropriate purpose).

Article 6

The business scope of the company is (fill in).

Article 7

The expected production of the company shall be as follows:

2006, value of output (fill in as appropriate)
2007, value of output (fill in as appropriate)

The environmental protection proposal on the selection of factory premise and the production procedure must be examined and approved by the environmental protection department of (name of government).

Article 8

The company may sell its products in the Chinese domestic market and in the international market, with its initially planned proportion of sales as follows:

For export (fill in percentage)
For the domestic market (fill in percentage)
or as permitted by WTO implementation.

Article 9

All of the materials necessary for production may be purchased in the Chinese market or the international market.

Chapter 3

Total amount of investment and registered capital

Article 10

The total amount of investment of the company is (fill in as appropriate).

Its registered capital is (fill in as appropriate).

The method of investment subscribed is (fill in cash or in kind as appropriate).

The method of investment subscribed shall comply with the *Implementing Regulations of Foreign Enterprise Law of the People's Republic of China.* The first payment shall be (fill in value) and shall be paid on or before (fill in date).

Article 11

Thirty days after the registered capital is paid, a Chinese registered accountant invited by the company shall verify it and provide a certificate of verification. The certificate of verification shall be submitted to the original examination approval authority and the industrial and commercial bureau.

Article 12

Within the term of the business, the company shall not reduce its registered capital.

Article 13

Any increase, assignment of the registered capital or alteration of major issues of the company shall be approved by the board of directors and submitted to the original examination approval authority for approval. The registration procedure for changes shall be dealt with at the original registration and administration office.

Chapter 4

Board of Directors

Article 14

The company shall establish the Board of Directors, which shall be the highest authority of the company and shall decide all major issues concerning the company and be responsible to the investor.

Article 15

The Board of Directors shall consist of a chairman and two directors appointed by the investor. The term of office for the directors is 3 years and they may be re-appointed. A written notice shall be submitted to the board when appointing or replacing directors. If unable to attend board meetings, directors may appoint a proxy with authorisation in writing.

Article 16

The chairman is a legal representative and an authorised signatory of the company, and shall manage the major issues of the company and supervise the Board of Directors.

Should the chairman be absent, the vice-chairman should call and preside, but should present a proxy in writing. The chairman and legal representative may appoint by power of attorney a representative to carry out itemised and specific duties on his behalf.

Article 17

The Board of Directors shall decide and supervise all major issues concerning the company. Its functions and powers are as follows:

1. Establishing and modifying the structure of the organisation and personnel plan
2. Deciding the engagement of senior management such as the General Manager, Vice General Manager, Chief Engineer, Chief Accountant, Auditor, etc. and their respective powers, duties and salaries
3. Deciding and approving the important reports submitted by the General Manager or the administration department
4. Amending the Articles of Association of the company
5. Approving annual financial reports and budgets

6. Drawing from the reserve fund, staff bonus and welfare fund
7. Deciding on the distribution plan of annual profits and method of covering any deficit
8. Drawing up labour contracts and major rules and regulations of the company
9. Discussing and deciding on the termination of production or merging with other organisations
10. Being in charge of termination or expiration of the company or its liquidation
11. Other major issues which shall be decided by the Board of Directors

Article 18

The Board of Directors shall unanimously agree upon the following issues:

1. Amendment of the Articles of Association of the company
2. Termination of the company
3. Increasing or transferring of registered capital of the company
4. Merging with another organisation or separation of the company or reformation of structure of the organisation.

Article 19

Issues except those listed in Article 18 shall be passed by a majority of votes.

Article 20

The Board of Directors shall convene a board meeting at least once a year. An interim meeting of the Board of Directors may be held based on a proposal of more than one third of the total number of directors. Board meetings shall be called by and presided over by the chairman. Should the chairman be absent, the vice-chairman shall call and preside over the meeting. Should any director be unable to attend the board meeting, he may present a proxy in writing to the board.

The quorum for a board meeting should be more than half of the directors. The board meeting will generally be held at the legal address of the company or at the address of the investor, or by telephone conference.

Article 21

The chairman shall give each director written notice 30 days prior to the date of routine board meetings. The notice shall cover the agenda, time and place of the meeting.

In the event an emergency board meeting is required, the chairman alone has the right to call such meeting at 24 h notice.

Article 22

After approval by the board, the minutes of each board meeting shall be signed by all attending directors, and the original thereof filed in the minute book of the company. The minute book shall be kept at the company's legal address unless otherwise required by the investor.

The language of record shall be in Chinese or Chinese and English.

The other issues that need to be discussed between sessions may be decided by appropriate means of communication and in writing. The resolution shall be valid.

Chapter 5

The Supervisor

Article 23

Companies established after January 1, 2006, shall have at least one Supervisor appointed by a meeting of the shareholders for a 3-year, (renewable) term of office.

The company's executive directors and senior management personnel shall not concurrently hold the Supervisor position.

The Supervisor (like the company directors) is not required to reside in or visit the PRC.

Article 24

The Supervisor shall have the following responsibilities:

1. checking the financial affairs of the company
2. supervising the duty-related acts of the directors and senior management personnel, and in the case that any violation of law, administrative regulation, Articles of Association or any resolution of the shareholders meeting has taken place, proposing their removal from the company
3. demanding that any director or senior management personnel make rectifications if his act has injured the interests of the company
4. attending the Board of Directors meetings and raising questions or suggestions on the matters to be decided by the Board of Directors
5. making investigations for the company—if the company is found to be running abnormally, and should it be deemed necessary, the supervisor may engage an accounting firm to assist in the ensuing investigations
6. other responsibilities provided for by Company Law and the Articles of Association.

Article 25

The expenses necessary for the Supervisor to perform his duties shall be borne by the company.

Chapter 6

Management organisation

Article 26

A management organisation shall be established in the company, with the General Manager responsible to the Board of Directors. It can consist of technology, marketing, finance and administration offices, etc., as appropriate.

Article 27

The company shall have one General Manager and one Deputy General Manager. The Deputy General Manager shall assist the General Manager in his work and the General Manager shall discuss the major issues with the Deputy General Manager.

Article 28

The General Manager is directly responsible to the Board of Directors. His powers are as follows:

1. Carry out resolutions of the Board of Directors
2. Organize and conduct the daily production, operation and management of the company
3. Represent the company to handle the daily business and production, appoint and remove administrative staff under authorisation of the Board of Directors
4. Other powers authorised by the Board of Directors.

Article 29

The term of office for the General Manager and the Deputy General Manager shall be 1 year, and may be renewed at the invitation of the Board of Directors. Unless terminated by the Board of Directors, the term of office for the General Manager and the Deputy General Manager, will be considered automatically renewed by period of 1 year. If it is not renewed, the Board of Directors shall give 3 months advanced notice.

Article 30

At the invitation of the Board of Directors, the chairman, vice chairman or directors of the board may concurrently hold the General Manager, Deputy General Manager or other senior management positions.

Article 31

The General Manager or Deputy General Manager shall not hold posts concurrently as General Manager or Deputy General Manager of other commercial organisations in commercial competition with their own company.

Article 32

In case any staff commits a serious dereliction of duty, they may be dismissed at any time upon the decision of the board. Those who violate the criminal law shall be under criminal sanction.

Article 33

The General Manager, Deputy General Manager, Chief Accountant and other senior management who wish to resign shall provide 30 days written notice to the Board of Directors.

Chapter 7

Financial and accounting

Article 34

The finance and accounting of the company shall be handled in accordance with laws of the PRC and the applicable regulations of the Ministry of Finance of the PRC and the situation of the company, which shall be submitted to the relevant finance department and tax department.

Article 35

The company should set up financial accounts and import and export goods accounts at its location, keep separate accounts and make accounting statements. The company should provide statistical data and make statistical statements according to the *Statistics Law of the PRC*.

Article 36

The fiscal year of the company shall coincide with the calendar year, i.e. from January 1 to December 31 on the Gregorian calendar. Any alteration of the fiscal year of the company because of special circumstances must have approval of the tax department.

Article 37

All vouchers, account books, statistic statements and reports of the company shall be written in Chinese. Copies may be made in English.

Article 38

The company shall use the accrual basis and both debit and credit accounts for its bookkeeping.

Article 39

The company shall prepare a balance sheet and a statement of income of the previous fiscal year before the end of each year. The financial statement shall be submitted to the original audit office and the administrative department of industry and commerce after being audited and certified by a certified auditor and upon instruction of the Board of Directors.

Article 40

The company adopts Renminbi (RMB) for its accounts. The cash, bank balance, other balance, debtor, creditor, income and expenses shall be recorded in original currency. The conversion of the RMB into other currency shall be in accordance with the exchange rate of the converting day published by SAFE.

Article 41

The company shall open accounts in RMB and foreign currency with the Bank of China or other banks agreed by SAFE.

Article 42

The following items shall be covered in the financial account books:

1. The amount of overall cash receipts and expense of the company
2. All material purchases and sales by the company
3. The registered capital and debts of the company
4. The time of payment, increase and assignment of the registered capital of the company.

Article 43

The annual accounting statement and liquidation accounting statement should be verified by a registered accounting office in China. The inspection report of accounts reported by the registered accounting office should be attached to the annual accounting statement and liquidation accounting statement.

Article 44

The company shall draw reserve funds, bonuses and welfare funds for staff and workers after payment of taxes. The Board of Directors decides the proportion of allocation. The reserve fund shall be used for making up losses, the proportion of which shall not be less than 5 percent of profits after tax payment. Upon termination of the WFOE licence period, the reserve fund shall be returned to the investors as an accrued asset.

Article 45

After paying taxes in accordance with the law and drawing the various funds, the remaining profits will be distributed every year according to the proportion of each shareholder's investment in the registered capital and according to the Board of Directors' resolution/decisions.

Article 46

The company shall not distribute profits unless the losses of previous fiscal year have been made up and the amount of the original investment has been returned to the parent company. Remaining profit from previous fiscal year can be distributed together with that of the current year. If the company enters into loan agreements with its parent, these may be repaid according to the agreement and at an interest rate 5 percent above the parent company's bank base rate at that time. Late payment shall incur charges of 1 percent interest on the full amount due compounded daily.

Article 47

The legitimate profits of the investor after paying income tax are allowed to be remitted out of China through the Bank of China or other banks in line with foreign exchange control measures.

Article 48

The salaries and other proper earnings after paying personal income tax of the foreign, overseas Chinese, Hong Kong and Macao workers and staff members are allowed to be remitted out of China through the Bank of China or other banks in line with foreign exchange control measures.

Chapter 8

Tax, foreign exchange control and insurance

Article 49

The company should pay all taxes required and enjoy tax reduction or tax exemption in accordance with the related and regulations of the PRC.

Article 50

The staff and workers of the Company should pay individual income tax according to the *Individual Income Tax Law of the PRC.*

Article 51

All matters concerning foreign exchange shall be handled in accordance with the *Provisional Regulations for Foreign Exchange Control of the PRC*, and other pertaining regulations.

Article 52

The company should keep the foreign exchange payment balance of its own accord.

Article 53

All insurances of the company should be provided by insurance corporations allowed to do business in China.

Chapter 9

Staff and trade union

Article 54

The required staff and workers will be selected through public selection and the company will employ those who are qualified in accordance with the *Labour Law of the PRC*.

Article 55

Both parties of employment and the labor contract should comply with The Labour Law of the PRC and other laws, regulations and provisions of Shanghai. A labour contract must include the following items:

1. The tasks or duties to be carried out
2. The duration of the labour contract
3. The working conditions
4. Salary, welfare benefits, labour insurance, labour protection, labour discipline
5. Conditions for determination of labour contract
6. The labour contract should be filed at the labour bureau. Employment procedures should be handled under its provisions.

Article 56

The company has the rights to take disciplinary action, record a demerit and reduce salary against those staff and workers who violate the rules and regulations of the company. In serious circumstances, they may be dismissed. Discharging of workers shall be filed with labour management department.

Article 57

The salary of the staff and workers shall be increased as appropriate to production growth and increases in the ability and skills of the staff.

Article 58

The staff and workers of the company have the rights to establish a trade union and carry out activities in accordance with the provisions of the *Trade Union Law of the PRC*.

Article 59

The trade union in the company is representative of the interests of the staff. The tasks of the trade union are:

1. To protect the democratic rights and material interests of the staff
2. To assist the company to arrange and make rational use of welfare funds and bonuses
3. To conciliate in labour disputes
4. To organise appropriate studies and activities
5. To educated staff to observe labour discipline and strive to fulfill the economic tasks of the company.

Article 60

The trade union will supervise the staff in the signing of labour contracts, or sign contracts on their behalf, and supervise the implementation of such contracts.

Article 61

The company shall allocate funds totaling 2 percent of all the salaries of the staff of the company as the trade union's funds, to be used by the trade union in accordance with the *Managerial Rules for the Trade Union Funds* formulated by the All Federation of Trade Union. The union shall present a budget for allocation of such funds to the Board of Directors for approval.

Chapter 10

Duration, termination and liquidation

Article 62

The duration of the company shall be 20 years, beginning from the day when the business license is issued.

Article 63

An application for the extension of duration shall be submitted to the original examination and approval authority 180 days prior to the expiry date. Only upon the approval may the duration be extended, the company shall go through registration formalities for the alteration at other appropriate bureaus and departments.

Article 64

The Board of Directors shall have the right to terminate the company in case one of the following situations occurs:

1. Expiration of the planned duration
2. The company suffers heavy losses

3. Natural calamities, war or other events which can not be prevented or avoided, in which the company suffers heavy losses and is incapable of continuing in business
4. Bankruptcy
5. The company is rescinded according to the law in case of violation of any applicable governmental laws, regulations, restrictions or prohibitions
6. The occurrence of other circumstances which are stipulated in the Article of Association

Article 65

In case the company is terminated before the term expires, it shall be submitted to the original examination and approval authority for approval.

Article 66

Upon the termination of the company, the Board of Directors shall set up a liquidation committee and liquidate the company's assets in accordance with the law of the PRC. Before the liquidation is completed, the investor shall not carry or remit funds aboard, and shall not dispose of the assets by itself.

Article 67

Upon completion of the liquidation, the company shall submit a liquidation report to the original examination and approval authority, go through the formalities for nullifying its registration in the original registration office and hand in its business license, and at the same time, make an announcement to the public.

Chapter 11

Rules and regulations

Article 68

Following are the rules and regulations formulated by the Board of Directors of the company:

1. Management regulations, including the powers and functions of the managerial branches and its working rules and procedures
2. Rules for the staff
3. System of labour and salary
4. System of work attendance record, promotion and awards and penalties for the staff
5. Rules on staff welfare
6. Financial system
7. Liquidation procedures upon the dissolution of the company
8. Other necessary rules and regulations.

Chapter 12

Supplementary articles

Article 69

Any amendment to the Articles of Association shall be unanimously agreed upon and decided by the Board of Directors and submitted to the original examination and approval authority for approval.

Article 70

The Articles of Association are written in Chinese and English.

Article 71

When the Articles of Association contravene the laws and regulations of the PRC, the latter shall prevail.

Article 72

The Articles of Association shall come into effect upon the approval of (fill in government authority).

Article 73

The Articles of Association is signed in (location), China, by the authorised representatives of the investor on (date).
Investor (stamp and chop)
Legal Representative (sign)
(date), in.

Summary

It is important to note that these articles are the basic English draft commonly provided by investment zones or government agents. As such they are not definitive and have not been modeled to take into account your businesses actual needs. This is why you need to take professional advice when structuring this document. It is also important to recognize that the finished articles need to be translated into Chinese and submitted as part of the applications approval process—meaning you need an accurate translation as Chinese language takes preference over English. We have seen occasions whereby basic draft Chinese, yet re-worked English articles had been submitted together as a corporate application—all to no avail as the Chinese language version takes priority.

6 The Application Process: Manufacturing WFOE

The application process to create a WFOE can be divided into two parts:

- Pre-registration—what happens *before* the WFOE formally exists
- Post-registration—what happens *after* the WFOE formally exists

This is done at the provincial or municipal level (e.g. Guangdong Province, Shanghai Municipality, Beijing Municipality, etc), albeit with input from local offices of state-level authorities. In addition, the five Special Economic Zones in South China have independent approval authority over this issue.

We now explain this in more detail; please also refer to the flowchart on the next page.

Pre-registration

Name registration

The relevant authority is the SAIC. This bureau administers the registration of all kinds of enterprises (including FIEs), organisations or individuals that are engaged in business activities; examines and ratifies the registration of business names; and reviews, approves and issues business licenses. Verification of feasibility of the proposed name by SAIC will take a few working days.

Only the Chinese name will be legally binding—the English name is not legally relevant for Chinese authorities. The word "China" cannot be freely included in the Chinese name. The name can be translated from English by meaning and/or phonetically.

Feasibility Study Report

We explained the background to this earlier.

Environmental Protection Valuation Report

This is intended to control manufacturing production processes according to specified environmental norms. The bureau will require information about the raw materials used, the machinery and equipment, consumption and safe disposal of toxic products. Please note that all assembly and manufacturing WFOEs applications shall obtain approval by this bureau. In some cases, a full report on the environmental impact issued by an appointed agent shall be required (for example in the chemical or leather processing business) and this may represent a major step to go through as it would affect the time-frame to get your factory up and running.

Issuance of Approval Certificate and Business License

The authorities will issue the Approval Certificate and Business License after assessing the following documentation:

From the Investor

- business license (certificate of incorporation—please note that depending upon locations, this may need to be notarised in the investor country of origin then translated into Chinese)
- bank statement to demonstrate credit worthiness (from relevant bank in country of origin then translated into Chinese)
- photocopy of passport of the Legal Representative of the investor company

From the New WFOE

- about the new business—name of the company, business scope, registered capital, business term, lease contract
- about the Legal Representative—photocopy of passport and passport size photos
- about the directors—CVs, photocopy of passport and passport size photos
- Feasibility Study Report
- Articles of Association
- Environmental Protection Valuation Report

The Certificate of Approval will be issued by the local office of the Ministry of Commerce. After the ministry issues the Certificate of Approval, there is a 30-day limit for the registration of the WFOE with the local office of the SAIC, who then issues the Business Licence.

After that step the WFOE now legally exists.

Post-registration

However, the paperwork does not stop there. You still have quite a bit to do before you have a fully functioning WFOE. This consists of:

1. Approval for making chops issued by Public Security Bureau
2. Enterprise Code registration with the Technical Supervision Bureau
3. Office inspection by the tax bureau and tax registration
4. Applying for a RMB bank account opening permit from the People's Bank and opening RMB bank account

Establishing Work Process Flow for Manufacturing Wholly Foreign Owned Enterprises in China
(please note variations may occur regionally and in specific industries requiring additional licensing)

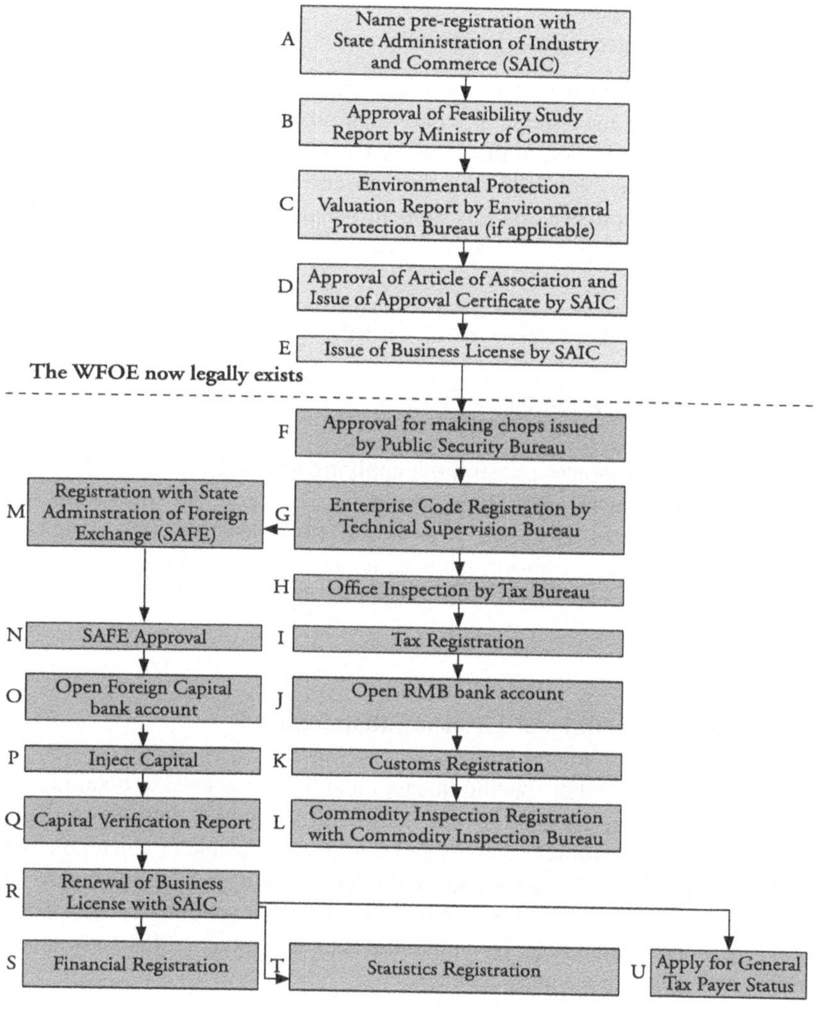

Procedural Timeframe: Typically three-four months from commencement to license issuance - depending on specific licensing complexities within certain industries.

5. Customs registration
6. Commodity inspection with Commodity Inspection Bureau
7. Registration with the State Administration of Foreign Exchange
8. Opening foreign capital bank account

9. Injection of capital and capital verification report
10. Renewal of business licence by SAIC after capital has been injected
11. Financial registration
12. Statistics registration
13. Application for general tax payer status

Please note many consultants and law firms do not regard post-registration procedures as part of their scope of work when processing client's applications—so either shop around for a firm that does, or ensure you have this vital component catered for elsewhere. Not following through correctly on these procedures can lead you to non-compliance and government penalties later on.

Other Pre- and Post-registration Issues to Consider

Corporate Name Translations

When applying for business registration, applying for trademark registrations and so on, it is important to spend time to obtain an appropriate translation of the company name, and to try to use it as a uniform translation. It is your corporate identity in China. A uniform Chinese name will be good for marketing and will also avoid troubles later with on-going documentation and application procedures.

Under-estimating Additional Licencing Requirements

Certain WFOEs have other specific licenses that they may need to obtain in order to operate. These can often be far more difficult to process and obtain than the original licence! For example, import and sale of consumable products, trading of certain metals, rare earths and so on, fuel, pharmaceuticals, etc. all require additional licensing applications , and you should ensure that you fully understand their processing procedures in order for you to dovetail all regulatory demands into your business operations in a timely manner.

7 The Application Process—Service WFOE and FICE

This is broadly similar to that for manufacturing WFOEs—refer to the flowchart on the next page.

Procedural Workflow for Establishing a Service WFOE or FICE in China
(please note regional variations and certain industry specifics may affect this)

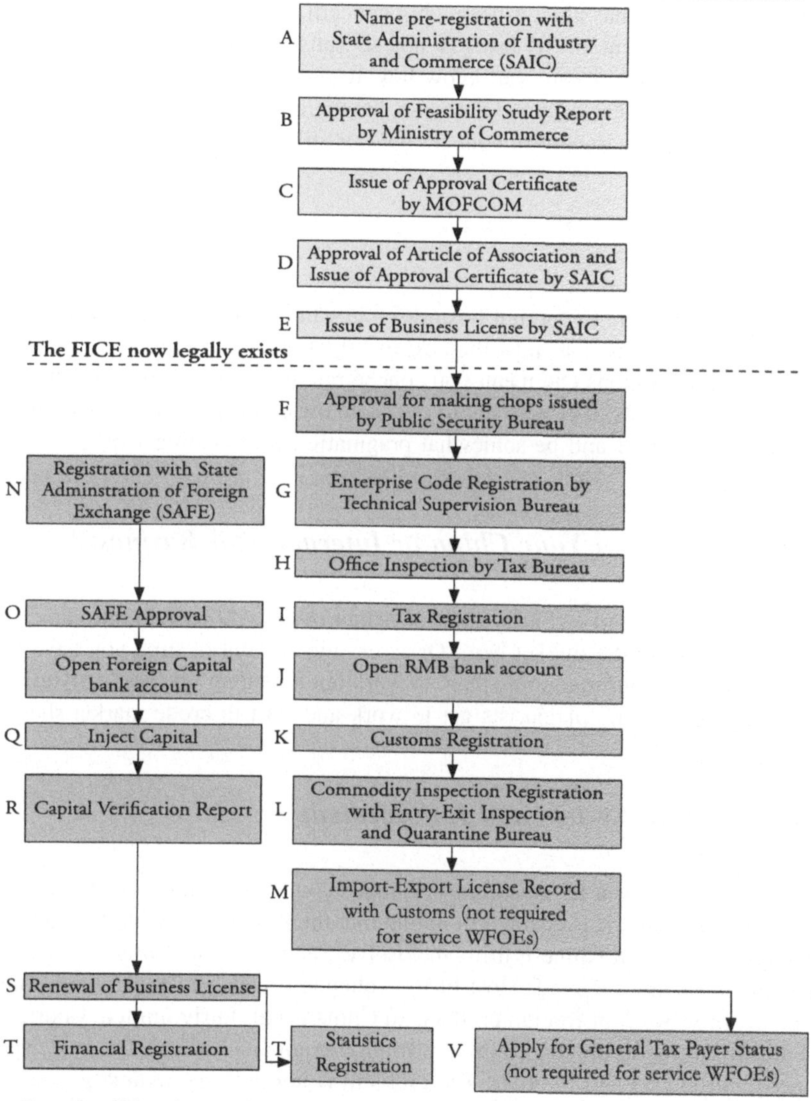

Procedural Timeframe: The process typically takes three-four months depending upon specific complexities from commencement to license issuance for it to be considered and properly planned.

8 Intellectual Property

Intellectual property has always been a big concern for foreign investors in China. Since the enforcement of IP laws is not so satisfactory at present, it is very important for foreign investors to know how to protect their intellectual property before any infringement occurs. Of course, having a WFOE rather than a JV does make it easier for you to control your IP, but it is still an issue to take into account.

Is it Worth it?

IP is an emotive issue to foreign businesses in China. But it is also important to assess the actual damage against the cost of litigation and emotions. Lawyers are expensive, and emotions can mean you concentrate more on the litigation than the case actually warrants. It is wise not to overstate the damage caused to your firm if you do get ripped off and be somewhat pragmatic about dealing with it.

Is Your IP Vital to Your China or International Business?

If it is, you may need to seriously assess whether or not you wish to introduce your technology at all to the market here. Or assess the amount of time you have with your IP as part of your marketing plan, to work out how long you are likely to have a free range before the plagiarists get to work and start to erode market share.

IP in the Legal System and Enforcement

Despite some comment to the contrary, China's courts are improving in upholding claims of plagiarism. It is also worth noting that the vast majority of infringements in China are between Chinese firms themselves, and it is not purely international firms that are being targeted. Most of the valuable brands in China are of course Chinese—mass sales of foreign products in China is still fairly limited. Courts can and do, in the main, uphold claims by foreign companies where the evidence is properly introduced and in order. The problem is not with the judiciary, although they are not perfect either. The main issue is that of enforcement—actually stopping the infringement once a judgment in your favour has been awarded.

Trademarks

You may believe that because you have already registered your trademark elsewhere, it is covered automatically in China. China is signatory to all the international protocols that the international community has drawn up concerning the registration and protection of international IP. Therefore, China follows the same system as most nations follow.

This includes registration of your mark. International recognition is only granted provided your mark has previously been registered in five other jurisdictions (thus proving its "international" status) or can be otherwise argued as an "internationally recognized brand"—which is a debatable point and subject to legal interpretation. This means if you have only registered your mark in your home country, you are not covered in China. For practical purposes however, even if you have international protection, we still recommend registering in China as courts may have difficulty in recognising international protocols if they are not used to them, and this will mean more time and expense in legal fees to educate the court and provide evidence of the significance of such protocols and China's adherence to them. Trademark registration in any event is inexpensive and should be undertaken as a matter of good business sense.

Patents

Patent infringement is becoming more and more common, and combatting this is a major challenge for foreign companies. When you come to China, you need to consider how to ensure your competitors will not pirate your key technologies. Patent application will be the first step. Careful drafting of the application will help your patent to be approved by the patent authority without too many changes, so you can enjoy the broadest protection allowed by law. In many patent lawsuits, the patentee loses the case simply because of the bad wording of the claims. Therefore, it is very important to find a professional, reliable professional firm to take care of your patent application.

Patents are further classified into inventions, utilities models and designs under Chinese Patent Law. The official fees for patent application will vary depending on the specific application and the category, for both the initial registration and renewal. Invention patents are for 20 years, and a utility model or design for 10 years. Unlike trademarks, once the period of validity of a patent expires, it cannot be renewed.

As mentioned, China is signatory to various international protocols when it comes to registrations of patents and trademarks. There is, however, a hole in the registration procedure for patents, which require they be registered and placed on public file for assessment prior to the patent being recognised as your own intellectual property. This means some entrepreneurial types scan such registrations specifically to steal designs and then immediately get into production even while your patent pending process is still on-going. This is not a China issue—it is a weakness in the international protocol of registrations and needs to be addressed in the fullest sense to protect expensive R&D and inventions from being used on the cheap by less scrupulous businesses.

Domain Names

With the rapid expansion of the Internet, more and more people have realised the importance of domain names. Usually, a company will register its trademark or its enterprise name as their domain name, and a good domain name ending in ".cn" will be very useful for marketing. Domain name registration follows the principle of first come, first served. It is very important to register the trademark/enterprise name before it is hijacked by others. A simple search of your company name or trademark on the Internet will show the importance of a domain name. The annual fees for registering such a domain name are very low.

Trade Secrets

"Trade secrets" is a very broad concept, and it may include all the information and documents that will bring economic benefits to the company and that should be protected by the company—this will include client information, price, design, production methods and procedures, programmes, etc. Trade secrets should not only be protected from competitors, but also amongst key personnel of the company.

Once your company is in the position of negotiation (e.g. for joint venture setup or an OEM contract) with another party and you need to disclose some of your trade secrets, be sure to sign a confidentiality agreement with the other parties and clearly show them what you are sharing as trade secrets.

For key personnel in charge of your trade secrets, a confidentiality agreement and sometimes also a non-competition agreement are also recommended. However, since non-competition agreements also fall within the scope of labor law, it is very important for the company to make sure that all the clauses in the non-competition agreement are in compliance with employment laws.

IP Management System

Intellectual property protection is very professional and complicated work. We suggest your company should have a person in charge of its IP related matters, building and keeping files, coordinating with external IP counsels, monitoring of the IP status, etc.

It will also be helpful to educate your employees to improve their IP consciousness, especially the sales people who are most familiar with the market and the distribution of fake products. Good communication with your clients will also help you to find clues on infringement.

WFOE Conversions and Closures

WFOEs also need to be established when other legal entities in China change due to an acquisition (in the case of JVs) or upgrades of contractual arrangements (processing agreements for exports to fully-fledged operations). This requires a somewhat different approach, as instead of a completely new incorporation, an already existing legal entity is being amended to evolve into a WFOE structure. In this chapter we also include other related issues, such as relocating a WFOE (which can occur, especially as part of some M&A transactions), the establishment of branches, and liquidation.

1 Converting Processing and Assembly Operations (LLJGs) to WFOES

Processing and Assembly Operations have accounted for a significant part of China's exports and have been particularly popular amongst Hong Kong and Taiwanese investors since the early 1980s. Under this arrangement, the Chinese party (either a local Chinese company or an FIE) processes materials or assembles parts supplied from abroad by the foreign party, and then ships the completed products back to the foreign party. No local sales are allowed and the whole production must be exported.

PRC laws allow for two structures for the importation of material/components to be processed in China for exports of final products—*jin liao jia gong* or JLJG and *lai liao jia gong* or LLJG.

The key distinction between the two structures lies in the title of the materials and finished products. Under a LLJG, the title to the raw materials is under the name of the foreign investor—the raw materials enter the PRC on a consignment basis and the title to all the raw materials and the finished products remains with

C. Devonshire-Ellis et al. (eds.), *Setting Up Wholly Foreign Owned Enterprises in China*, China Briefing, DOI: 10.1007/978-3-642-15540-6_3,

the contractor outside China. The foreign party would normally pay the Chinese party a set fee for each unit produced.

Under a JLJG arrangement, the WFOE in China purchases the raw materials from its overseas suppliers for its own account and the title of the goods is passed on to the WFOE. The WFOE would then sell to the previous supplier the finished products at a margin.

Recent Developments

Over time, foreign investors have increasingly found themselves in the position of having, on the one hand, still to cater for the overseas markets but also, on the other hand, to tap into the growing domestic market. In fact, both local Chinese companies as well as FIEs were increasingly demanding locally manufactured goods of high standards for which they could easily pay for in local currency. This has triggered a flow of first and second tier manufacturers who in the past focused only on processing trade turning their attention to the domestic market. At the present moment, some of them are not only able to still manufacture for export under the old LLJG arrangements, but can also provide local supplies to their Chinese clients. Legal and market changes have also made it easier for WFOEs to sell locally without having to export the majority of their production.

So, What Does this All Mean?

In a nutshell, you can set up your WFOE operations in China, allowing you:

- to carry out processing and assembly contracts in the PRC through the importation of raw materials, components and equipment free of duties and VAT
- to sell your manufactured products locally to your clients, provided you stay within your approved business scope. These two activities, of course, have to be kept separate in term of logistics within the factory, as "bonded" materials and related final goods and other products manufactured should be clearly kept apart.

Advantages and disadvantages of establishing a WFOE versus processing and assembly operations
The advantages are:

- greater flexibility and control over production
- exports processing activities still possible
- local sales also available

- reduced holding company overheads and administration costs
- income kept offshore and payments arranged to the WFOE based on the actual working capital required
- convenient for group consolidated cash and margins arrangements.

The disadvantages are:

- capital contribution required
- administration and management structure in the PRC
- possible "transfer pricing" issue.

There are also a number of issues you need to consider in terms of establishment, operations and tax—see the table.

Key Issues to Consider When Switching from LLJG to WFOE

You need to think about the following:

- timing—you should do your homework in terms of reducing the production stoppage to the bare minimum—something which may come as a consequence of restructuring your operations
- applying for the WFOE licenses

as well as:

- applying to customs for exemptions on Customs Duties for imported equipments, including second-hand equipment and equipment still under customs supervision
- transforming the original unvalued and "bonded" imported equipment of the LLJG operations to the registered capital of the new WFOE. Attention should be paid to the nature of the operations, the category of investment it belongs to and the "customs status" of the previously imported equipment. Depending on the time such equipment has already been used in the PRC, different tax considerations may apply, from complete exemption to payment of Custom Duties and VAT
- considering whether the new WFOE should possess the production equipment before it is allowed to apply to customs for importation of components and raw materials
- terminating the LLJG contract(s) and writing off the tax registrations and the business license accordingly

Do your due diligence to make sure that the premises you are renting have all the permissions in place—the factory you are currently using for LLJG operations cannot necessarily give you a WFOE license—and if you have any doubts take professional advice.

Issue	Item	WFOE	LLJG
WFOEs vs LLJGs—comparison list for establishment, operation and tax			
Establishment	Minimum registered capital	Around RMB100,000 for single shareholder companies and RMB30,000 for multiple shareholder companies, with regional variations	N/A
	Type of company	Foreign-invested enterprise	Chinese domestic company
	Legal representative	The foreign investor	The Chinese partner
	Timescale for set up	90–120 days	About 15 days
	Operational term	10–50 years	Less than 10 years
Operations	Land and building use rights	Under the name of the WFOE or holding company	The real property will belong to the Chinese factory under the name of LLJG
	Raw materials	Purchased from local or overseas supplier	Processed as materials belonging to foreign investor
		No custom duty and VAT applicable for overseas purchases by using customs handbook	
		Pay the VAT and get the refund after export sales for local purchase	No custom duty and VAT but a deposit may be required
	Sales	No output VAT for export sales	Processed as materials belonging to foreign investor
		17% output VAT for domestic sales and can get the reduction in input VAT	
	Income	All exports/local sales	Set processing fee
	Fixed assets	Can be mortgaged to get bank loans	Cannot be mortgaged to get bank loans

Issue	Item	WFOE	LLJG
Tax	VAT	The normal rate is 17% based on the increased value	6% on the processing fee, tax exemption available
		Tax system of "exemption, set-off & refund" is practiced for the exports sales	
		Imported equipment should pay 17% VAT based on the equipment value	
	Corporate income tax	If the annual export sales account for more of 70% of the annual output, a reduced corporate income tax applies	
Tax	Individual income tax	From 5 to 45% based on monthly salary	From 5 to 45% based on monthly salary
	Management fee	N/A	Typically 18 to 25% as processing fees paid to the local government/local factory
	Customs duties	Imported equipment should pay custom duties based on the equipment value if the WFOE license mentions local sales	A deposit is required for the raw materials and equipment during the processing/operation period
		Imported raw materials should pay the custom duty/VAT if the final products are sold domestically. Custom duty/VAT does not apply if all the final products are exported and customs handbook is used	

2 Converting Joint Ventures to WFOEs

Converting your existing JV to a WFOE is essentially a re-registration procedure that is reasonably straightforward to accomplish. However, the following must be first taken into consideration:

- is the industry that you are in a non-restricted activity that does not require a Chinese partner (see earlier section on encouraged industry status)?
- is the mechanism for purchase or transfer of shares adequately catered for in the JV articles?

Valuation of Shares and Assets

Point one is a review of the articles and a look at the mechanism for transfer. This may involve a valuation of the business, in which case both parties need to agree on this. Local valuation firms may not be entirely impartial. If you can, insist upon an independent valuer with international experience. Ideally, the preferred list of valuers should have been specified in the articles from the outset. Often there are no such articles and a board resolution to appoint a specific firm may need to be negotiated and passed.

Board Resolutions

Assuming that a price has been agreed, further unanimous board resolutions need to be passed resolving to convert the JV to a WFOE. Usually these will tie in with an agreement over transfer of capital to purchase the equity, which then triggers the share transfer.

Re-registration

Once this has been accomplished, it is a relatively straightforward process of submitting a new set of articles of association to the original licensing authority (whichever local government approved the original JV). These should include of course reference to the new set of laws (WFOE) that govern the activities of fully funded business, a new board of directors, and possibly other managerial positions as well.

One advantage of converting JV's to WFOEs is that there may not be a requirement to inject any further capital into the business, as the JV will of course have already been essentially capitalised.

Once the new set of documents is filed, the old JV chops and licenses are handed back to the authorities and the new structure is registered in its place. New chops, licenses and other pertinent certificates are issued and away you go. It is possible to keep operations intact and on-going during this process as it is not in anyone's interest for the business to have any down time—this would mean a loss of tax revenues for the local government!

Consolidated Tax Breaks

One area that can prove awkward is if this occurs with converting multiple JV's in different locations that have been enjoying tax breaks, but which are not in synchronisation as regards time span. This will need to be negotiated with the new tax authority in the new location, who will require to see the relevant tax bureau documents from other locations prior to making a decision. Regional tax bureaus are usually fair when it comes to reevaluating multiple tax breaks and consolidating these into one—it just takes a bit of time and patience in explaining the intricacies of the previous holidays.

Acquiring Staff

Be aware that if you convert to a WFOE, your pension fund or redundancy liabilities are extended back to the time when you first formed the JV—not from day one of the converted WFOE. Have a look at your human resource issues beforehand if acquiring numerous staff—especially if having to make redundancies or planned layoffs later. It can get expensive.

Summary

Most of the problems encountered with conversion are inadequate provisions catering for this in the original articles. These of course can be amended but will need to be done beforehand to allow a smooth transition. A review is a prerequisite.

3 Relocating WFOEs

WFOEs can be relocated, and occasionally are under some M&A structures. The main issues facing a relocation are as follows:

- agreement to redeploy existing staff in a new location or to provide severance
- consolidation of any existing tax breaks in a specific location that need to be added to or folded into a new locale or entity
- repayment or settlement of any incentives provided that will not now be fully realized given the relocation
- customs clearance issues over the transfer of goods/property held in a bonded area

Relocations may additionally require the merger of one WFOE into another, again this can be accomplished and is mainly a tax consolidation, customs and human resources issue. Local government negotiations need to be handled with some sensitivity as they are losing tax revenues, employment and perhaps prestige, however legally speaking WFOEs may be moved and merged. These are obviously somewhat complicated bespoke administrative matters to execute and vary on a case by case basis; you will need to take professional advice from a reputable firm experienced in this field in order to proceed with such plans.

4 Establishing WFOE Branches

Chinese law allows a WFOE to set up one or more branches. These can be used to expand territorially without the need to set up another fully fledged PRC company. By expanding in this way, your WFOE can delocalise production, sales and marketing to cover virtually any region in China and provide a better service tailored to local customer needs.

There is, however, often confusion between a Representative Office and a WFOE branch. These are very different entities.

An RO is the liaison office of a foreign company, incorporated outside mainland China (including Hong Kong, Macau and Taiwan). An RO cannot issue invoices and cannot sign a commercial contract.

A WFOE branch, on the other hand, is the liaison/operational office of a foreign invested company that is already incorporated in mainland China, under the control of the China based head office of the WFOE. It can do business within (but not beyond) the same business scope as its head office, and can issue invoices and sign commercial contracts. In addition, the WFOE branch keeps separate accounts from the head office.

However, it is *not* an independent legal entity—it cannot usually bear liabilities on its own. Of course, this also implies it needs no additional registered capital to balance—although the head office WFOE is required to be fully capitalised before it can set up branches.

Note there are also some special branch companies which would bear liabilities (and require corresponding additional registered capital) on their own, e.g. a branch of a bank.

The application process for setting up a branch is very similar to that for a fully fledged WFOE.

5 WFOE Liquidations

According to PRC law, if a company experiences financial difficulties and the board deems it necessary to dissolve the company, or the company is unable to carry out its business in a manner acceptable to the board of directors, the board of directors, upon a unanimous board resolution, can apply for approval from the competent approval authority for such termination. Once approval is obtained, the company can commence liquidation procedures. The process is as described below.

The procedures to close a WFOE are no easier or shorter than they are to set up such a company, and normally take between 6 and 9 months to complete.

Creation of a Liquidation Committee

1. If the company is to be terminated upon approval of the competent authority, the board shall appoint a liquidation committee
2. The liquidation committee shall liquidate and value the company's assets in accordance with PRC law and the Articles of Association
3. The liquidation committee shall consist of at least three members appointed by the board and shall include the chairman and the general manager. Qualified professional advisors, such as certified public accountants, may also be appointed as members or appointed to assist the liquidation committee. The chairman shall be the chairman of the liquidation committee, and another member may be appointed as the vice-chairman.
4. The liquidation committee shall have the right to terminate employment contracts, to sell, export, transfer, assign or otherwise dispose of any and all assets belonging to the company whether they be inside or outside the PRC, as well as to conclude all business matters of the company, in accordance with PRC law and the principles set out in the Articles of Association.
5. The liquidation committee shall conduct a thorough examination of the company's assets and liabilities, and shall develop a liquidation plan, which, if approved by the board, shall be executed under the liquidation committee's supervision.
6. If the company's assets and/or business must be sold, the liquidation committee shall endeavor to obtain the highest possible price for the company's assets and/or business.
7. The liquidation committee shall exercise the following functions and powers during liquidation:

(a) liquidate the assets of the company, prepare a balance sheet and list of assets, and formulate the liquidation plan
(b) make an announcement for the benefit of unknown creditors and notify known creditors in writing

(c) complete any unfinished business of the company
(d) submit the appraisal and valuation of assets and the basis for calculation
(e) pay all outstanding taxes
(f) pay all outstanding debts in full
(g) settle all of the company's claims and debts
(h) dispose of the remaining assets after the company's debts have been settled
(i) represent the company in any civil litigation
(j) produce the liquidation report and submit it to the board of directors and competent approval authority for approval.

Liquidation Audits

Liquidation audits are generally required twice in the process:

- when the termination application is submitted to related authorities and the application is approved by authority
- when all termination procedures have been completed.

In addition to issues covered in normal audit procedures, liquidation audits focus on these additional issues:

- the financial performance of the company in the 6 months prior to the date of declaring liquidation
- the completeness and truth of information on assets, such as:
  - whether the calculation of accounts receivable is correct
  - whether the bad debts write-off was properly authorised
  - whether the bank account records are complete
  - whether physical assets properly belong to the company
  - whether disposal/loss of fixed assets is approved by related authorities
  - whether investing assets are recorded and distributed correctly
- the liabilities of the company, such as:
  - whether salaries payable are calculated correctly
  - whether tax payable has been cleared properly
  - whether other liabilities have been cleared properly
- the amount of the liquidation expenses and whether they were spent in compliance with the law.

Liquidation Deadlines

The liquidation committee shall observe the following deadlines:

- within 7 days of beginning the liquidation, the relevant authorities must be notified
- within 10 days of establishing the liquidation committee, it must notify known creditors and ask them to declare their claims
- within 10 days of establishing the liquidation committee, it must release an announcement in both a national newspaper and a local provincial or municipal newspaper. Within 60 days of establishing the liquidation committee, it shall make at least one additional public announcement.

Distribution of Liquidated Proceeds

In accordance with PRC law, revenues from the sale or disposal of the liquidated assets shall be paid out in the following order:

(a) liquidation expenses, including remuneration to members of and advisors to the liquidation committee
(b) wages, labor insurance premiums and welfare benefits of employees
(c) outstanding taxes
(d) outstanding secured debts
(e) other outstanding debts.

After payments have been made in accordance with provisions above and upon completion of the liquidation procedures, the remaining revenue shall be converted into US$, or any other foreign currency acceptable to the investor through a designated foreign exchange bank or any other method permitted by PRC law, and shall be freely remitted or transported abroad.

Cancellation of Registration

Upon completion of the liquidation procedures, the liquidation committee shall submit the liquidation report, approved by the board, to the approval authority, and return its business license and cancel its registration with the relevant government authorities including the Ministry of Commerce, State Administration of Industry and Commerce (SAIC), the customs administration, the taxation authorities and State Administration of Foreign Exchange (SAFE). All the company's bank accounts shall be closed.

The investor shall have the right to preserve the originals of all accounting records and business documents of the company.

Within 10 days from the submission of the liquidation report, the company should perform deregistration with the authorities, and upon completion of the deregistration, the company can repatriate the remaining funds back to the investor. These deregistrations are:

- deregistration from MOFCOM, and cancellation of the Approval Certificate
- tax audit and deregistration from local tax bureau
- tax audit and deregistration from state tax bureau
- customs deregistration
- deregistration with SAFE
- deregistration from SAIC
- deregistration of Business Code Certificate
- public announcement in a newspaper to terminate the business
- remit funds back to investors
- close bank accounts.

Development Zones

An important part of your WFOE business plan is clearly answering the question of exactly where in China you will set it up. China is a huge country, and if you have flexibility it is almost always worth considering several options. Costs, infrastructure and markets vary widely from north to south, east to west, as the country is not all at the same level of development.

Of course in some cases you may be forced to go to a particular location, for example if you are following a partner company into China or have very specific business needs. But for the purposes of this discussion we will assume you want to explore several alternative places.

Like most developing countries, China still offers a number of tax and other advantages for foreign investors. These can be quite significant and you need to understand what is available that may suit your business plans.

Since the early 1980s, following the opening up of the Chinese economy, development zones began appearing in China. Their success largely stems from the preferential policies they offer and the safe investment environment they create. They do tend to share advantages such as convenient locations, modern developed infrastructure, rich human resources and efficient management and services.

Often the name differences refer to duty levels and import/export restrictions. But the differences can be, by far, greater than the similarities. For manufacturing investors in China, choosing a development zone as their base is the first step in an enormous risk-hedging exercise. Most consider at least three, or as many as five. As every zone has a personality of its own, it is essential to look beyond the pamphlets and the published information, and get down to the details.

The key points to consider, however, will still be whether the added value brought by location, local administration and services and tax rebates will justify an operation in dearer development zones. Quality and supply of infrastructure, labor availability, proximity to local suppliers and major transport infrastructures are also major issues to be considered prior to any commitment. Also remember that land purchase costs and premises rents are negotiable even within the same

C. Devonshire-Ellis et al. (eds.), *Setting Up Wholly Foreign Owned Enterprises in China*, China Briefing, DOI: 10.1007/978-3-642-15540-6_4,

zone, and it is thus advisable to shop around to find a suitable location before deciding to invest in a special zone. Infrastructure charges vary too.

Also, readers should be aware that the Ministry of Land and Resources and other government departments concluded an unprecedented nationwide probe into rampant land abuses in development zones in 2003. The investigation resulted in the shutting-down of 4,735 development zones, about 70 percent of the nation's total, and some policy restraint on expansion remains in place. Most problems arose at the level of provincial zones.

Investors should ensure, particularly with provincial and municipal level zones, that the zone authorities have appropriate central government permission for all the incentives that they offer.

In addition, China's accession to the WTO may lead to a changing role for such zones, as distinctions between incentives for foreign and domestic firms, and tariffs and non-tariff barriers begin to disappear. However, they are unlikely to disappear completely—most of the zones are well located geographically for international trade and can offer a level of service to investors above that of non-zone areas, and many are beginning to specialize in particular industries.

China currently has just over 2,000 development zones, covering around 13,700 km^2 of land. The main types of *state-level zone* are described below. In addition, there are also many municipal and provincial level zones, amongst other types.

Readers should be aware that the titles of many Chinese zones can be expressed in several different ways in English, adding confusion as to which is which and what type they are.

See the website of the China Association of Development Zones (http://www.cadz.org.cn/en/) for more details of the major state-level zones.

The main state-level types and their characteristics are as follows.

Special Economic Zones (SEZ)

- first type of Chinese DZ, dating from early 1980s. All are located in south China in Shenzhen, Shantou, Xiamen, Zhuhai, and Haikou
- aimed at a wide spectrum of industry
- the five cities retain rights to enact their own relevant legislation without reference to their provincial government
- closed areas for which nationals from other regions may require a special permit to visit.

Economic and Technological Development Zones (ETDZ)

- 90 nationwide—every province, municipality and autonomous region has at least one, coastal areas have several each—the earliest date from 1982 to 1984, later spread inland

- tend to be aimed at technology-intensive industry and to focus on several key sectors each
- many now include Export Processing Zones (see below)
- Economic and Technological Development Zones (ETDZ) authorities can approve FIEs with a value of up to US$30 million and can guide investment by locally made regulations.

High-tech Industrial Development Zones (HIDZ)

- 67 nationwide, every province has at least one (except Tibet, Ningxia, Qinghai)—they date from 1990s
- sometimes known as New and High-Technology DZs, High Tech Parks or New Districts
- they are aimed primarily at commercializing the results of scientific research, and thus encourage industries such as IT, electronics, pharmaceuticals, new materials, etc.—they are all part of the "Torch" programme of scientific development and are often located next to universities

Free Trade Zones (FTZ)

- 15 in total, all coastal obviously, next to ports, usually about 6–10 km^2, dating from 1990s
- "inside the territory, outside the Customs"—specialized areas for international trade and bonded operations within the area, with warehousing, bonded areas and logistics facilities
- various VAT, tax and other incentives
- many companies who are manufacturing for export are located in these zones
- also, until recently, the only area where one could create trading WFOEs.

Export Processing Zone (EPZ)

- 60 in all, many coastal, but many newer ones inland
- fairly new type of DZ—created since 2000, all around 2–3 km^2 or less, generally within an existing DZ, usually ETDZ
- simpler mechanism than Free Trade Zones for export processing.

Human Resources

This section explains some other general HR issues that you will need to take into account when establishing your WFOE. Please also refer to the tax chapter later in the book.

1 Employing Chinese Staff

Yes, it may be very useful to have that ever-so-nice-and-efficient local Chinese person help you with all aspects of setting up your China operations, including all business licences, offices, bank accounts, handling all documentation and so on. The language and bureaucracy are almost unintelligible and you are a busy corporate executive. But wait—is it normal business practice—anywhere—to have one person in control of all aspects of your country operations?

No, it is not. And with very good reason:

- their abilities may not stretch as far as international competencies—although they may in fact be honest and helpful, the way in which foreign companies have to be administered in China, and the reporting structures they have to go through, are very different from those that Chinese companies have to adhere to. In reality, foreign businesses in China face far more scrutiny than Chinese companies do. If your employee, good as he may be, is not familiar with the regulatory aspects concerning operating and maintaining an international office or business in China, chances are there will be issues on which your company will immediately be out of compliance. That can, and does, get expensive. Additionally, there are circumstances where the employee may deliberately keep the company out of compliance, to obtain benefits or other leeway later if any argument arises against their favour later on.
- having one person in control of all your corporate documents and/or banking—is it very common? The risks are obvious. You can lose all your abilities to

C. Devonshire-Ellis et al. (eds.), *Setting Up Wholly Foreign Owned Enterprises in China*, China Briefing, DOI: 10.1007/978-3-642-15540-6_5,

operate the company overnight if they decide to walk out of the door. Plus all your money.

- insertion of family and friends into your supply chain—this is very common. You need to audit your purchasing and sales departments regularly to ensure employees are not placing orders with companies owned by friends or relatives that are then charging your business at rates well over the market odds.
- setting up of parallel business—in one particularly nasty case we were called into investigate, two Canadian-Chinese were hired, having worked for the parent company overseas for several years, to establish a China manufacturing entity. This they did, however the China business was never able to attain anywhere like the projected sales, and had to be continuously funded from the parent to tide it over. A variety of "market conditions," "competitor pricing" and so on were given as excuses. When, just before a new US$1 million investment was to be injected into the China entity, the parent decided to just have a quick internal audit, things started to become clear. The two trusted employees had established a mirror company, with a similar sounding Chinese name to the international brand, and had been diverting all orders to that business instead. "Local competitive pricing" indeed. From a business the staff themselves had established to compete with their employers.

2 Employing Expatriate Staff

There are problems with expatriate staff as well.

- *hiring lawyers with no China experience*—expensive, and not really much point, especially if their Chinese language capabilities are minimal. However, many look good, and although their firms may have a China presence, what about their individual presence in China? International lawyers are great at international work—cross border structuring and so on—but far too many of them profess expertise in areas of China practice they are neither qualified nor experienced into be dealing with. Are you looking for a salesman selling his firm, or proper advice? Really, if you need to hire a lawyer with China experience—go to a firm that has the real thing. That is what they are there for, and China has had private lawyers now for 15 years—Google their names to see how well known they are.
- *hiring personnel on their language skills alone*—well, everyone has to start somewhere. But a new kid just out of language school is still a new kid out of language school, and will have no experience of the "China" issues. Do not expect miracles. And 2 years in China does not an expert make. Young graduates do have skills of course, but do not weigh them down too much with managerial responsibilities before they have had time to adjust to a commercial business environment and have found their feet around your business. A management development programme designed to maximise on their language skills yet

introduce them to your business will reap greater rewards both for you and for them if you treat them with continuing educational attention.

- *the China guys*—expats of note are those who really know their way around, and can steer you away from all the problems we have identified in this issue. They will have a good grasp of the language, and may well have settled down with family here. You cannot survive in China without knowing how to get on, and this is a matter of experience as well as possessing inherent patience, tenacity and people and communications skills. They are available—interestingly at this time, many of the established multinationals are localising and expatriate engineering and other talent is perhaps more available in China than ever before.

3 Good Recruitment Practice

This applies to all staff, irrespective of nationality. Just because "this is China," there is no reason not to incorporate the normal checks and balances that you would back home.

- check language skills, both oral and written—some Chinese staff have their friends write their English CVs for them, while many expats overstate the fluency of their Chinese. Note also that regional dialects can enhance or limit the ability of your staff to operate locally.
- check all backgrounds and references—often neglected and often regretted later. Follow up those qualifications and references. You are paying for them so make sure they are really part of the package.
- pay staff properly—if you want to retain them, pay them properly. Not just their welfare payments that you should be making in any event, but enough to keep them motivated and keen on continuing to work for you. China may be the current centre of cheap manufacturing—but there is no reason for you to be cheap when it comes to your staff. Or you will end up spending more time on recruitment operations than on your actual money-making operations.

4 General Conditions and Salaries

Working hours must be in accordance with the local regulations, which normally are 8 h per day and 40 per week (if overtime is required for special reasons, it must not exceed 3 h a day and the total overtime hours worked per month must not exceed 36 h). The company shall also cover for employee's welfare, normally including pension, medical insurance, unemployment and injury. For overtime payments, the labour law states that employees must not receive less than 150 percent of their normal wage for extensions of regular working days; not less than

200 percent for extensions on days of rest and not less than 300 percent for extension of statutory holidays.

In comparing labor costs in different cities across China, please note that in more inland or remote areas workers wages are comparatively lower but, at the same time, skilled staff may also be more difficult to find.

Professional staff are constantly searching for better opportunities, living conditions and higher remuneration, so expect to pay higher salaries to retain skilled junior and middle management. Once you start developing your organisation, you will also find out how high turnover could be a mounting problem to face, taking into consideration the fact that more and more companies are now rushing into the market and poaching good employees within similar industries and this has become a normal and frequent practice.

The company normally provides meals. You can budget for an internal canteen or simply subcontract the provision of meals to a third party. RMB10–12 per day per person seems to be a good estimate for one employee's daily breakfast/lunch/dinner expenses. Office staff often receive a similar allowance. Please note this figure, as it will amount to quite a sum every month for larger workforces!

Manufacturing companies also normally provides lodging, so budget for around RMB50–60 per person per month. We have seen up to 16 people crammed into a tiny cubicle. Be fair to your workforce and you will gain in terms of lower staff turnover and better attitude at work. The trade unions and the local media will not hesitate to highlight poor conditions.

Mandatory Welfare Payments

When calculating salaries, pay attention to the social insurance and housing funds. These are also mandatory along with pension and unemployment funds. Some investors seem to have no idea about these, even after taking professional advice elsewhere. You need to make mandatory welfare payments to your local staff, that is the law, and you need to budget for this. How much is dependent on your location as there are variants—some of them significant—on a national basis. As a general rule of thumb it will be an amount equivalent to between 30 and 60 percent of total salaries—so you need to know exactly how to cater for this and monitor the payment of it. Not factoring this expense into your registered capital will leave you short of money, with a very unhappy labor force, and possibly legal action to recover the monies due. Pay attention to this liability and budget for meeting it.

5 The Labor Contract Law

On Friday, June 29, 2007, China's top legislature, the National People's Congress adopted the Labor Contract Law which came into effect on January 1, 2008.

The Law protects workers' legal rights by demanding a written contract. If employers do not sign a written contract with their employees within a year after the employees start to work for them, it should be taken as that they have signed a labor contract of an unfixed term.

It is the country's first law governing the establishment, revision, and termination of labor contracts in the People's Republic of China. It is designed to mitigate against poor working conditions, minimise labor-management disputes, and stabilise the job market. Under the previous labor contract system, employers were able to terminate contracts without notice, withhold workers' wages, and refuse to renew contracts. The Law is decidedly pro-worker, and includes many provisions that protect laborers who are in a disadvantaged position in the market economy.

Some of the key points of the law are given in the following sections.

Fixed Term Contracts

- a written contract between the employer and employee is required; if no contract is provided then the employment relationship will commence from the employee's first day of work. A written contract should be signed within 1 month of starting work, and an employer who fails to provide such a contract after 1 month will be forced to pay the employee twice their monthly salary.
- the law only allows for two continuous fixed term contracts. Any further contracts must be, in general, open term contracts.

Payments

- an employer must pay severance, in the amount of one month's salary for each year served, to any employee whose fixed-term contract is not renewed, unless the employee rejects a new contract on equal or improved terms. If the employee's monthly salary is three times higher than the average monthly salary of the previous year for this region then the employer is only obligated to pay a severance equivalent to three times the average monthly salary for each year served.
- in cases of unlawful dismissal, the severance payment outlined for lawful dismissal is doubled to 2 months' salary for every year of service.

Mass Layoffs

- employers will be required to listen to the opinions of unions and/or employees regarding mass layoffs—defined as the laying off of 20 or more employees or no less than 10 percent of total staff—and give 30 days advance warning, under certain specific situations provided by law, i.e. if the company has been restructured according to the bankruptcy law; or where an employer adjusts the way in which the company carries out its business, changes the nature of the business or makes technology-based changes.

Non-competition Agreement

- employees who leave a company can be bound to a non-competition agreement for up to 2 years following termination, provided that corresponding economic compensation is paid to those employees on a monthly basis during the effective period of the non-competition.
- this may apply only for senior managers, senior technicians and other people who have knowledge of the trade secrets of the employer.

Probationary Period

- the maximum probation period is based on the term of the contract, thus:
  - 1 month, if contract term is less than 1 year
  - 2 months, if contract term is less than 3 years
  - 6 months, if contract term is more than 3 years
- however, where the labor contract has a specific purpose or is based on a specific project, this probationary period may not apply.
- employers shall pay their employees at least 80 percent of their contractual salaries during the probationary period. This figure shall not be lower than the minimum salary set by the government for this particular region or provided by the employer for the same position.

Labor Unions

- the role of labor unions has been strengthened. The previous laws, which require employers to notify labor unions prior to terminating a labor contract for any reason, are still in effect. Employers that do not have established labor unions are required to notify the union at the next higher level. Unions are also allowed to engage in collective bargaining and enter into collective contracts.
- a company is required to gain approval for its employee manuals, and company rules require a consultation with the labor union, workers' congress, or by workers' representative assembly or equal negotiation, before implementation
- if the labor union or an employee is of the opinion that a rule or regulation is inappropriate then it should be improved after consultation
- the labor bureau has the right to order an employer to change company rules that violate laws and administrative statues.

China's Business Taxes

1 Corporate Income Tax

On March 16, 2007, Chinese lawmakers passed the Corporate Income Tax Law, unifying the tax rates for foreign and domestic enterprises. The law, which took effect on January 1, 2008, brought China's tax laws more in-line with international standards. It has unified the two existing tax codes; one for domestic enterprises, the other for foreign-invested enterprises, into one and represents a fundamental change in China's tax policy.

The Corporate Income Tax Law contains general provisions as well as chapters on what constitutes taxable income, taxes payable, tax incentives, withholding tax at the source, special tax adjustments, administration of the levy and collection of taxes, as well as some supplementary provisions.

Corporate income tax is calculated against the net income in a financial year after deducting reasonable business costs and losses—in other words it is effectively a tax on profits. It is settled on an annual basis but is often paid quarterly with adjustments either refunded or carried forward to the next year. The final calculation is based on the year-end audit.

The income tax rate for all companies in China, both foreign and domestic, is 25%. Industry-based tax incentives exist which reward enterprises involved in the high or new technology sectors.

Tax rate	Applicable enterprises
Standard rate 25%	Most enterprises
Reduced rate 20%	Small and low-profit enterprises
Withholding income tax 20%	Foreign enterprises without permanent establishment in China but who derive income from China

C. Devonshire-Ellis et al. (eds.), *Setting Up Wholly Foreign Owned Enterprises in China*, China Briefing, DOI: 10.1007/978-3-642-15540-6_6,

Tax Incentives

A number of tax incentives exist:

- Qualified advanced technological service enterprises are eligible for a reduced income tax rate of 15 percent in 21 model cities
- "Encouraged" high-tech enterprises are eligible for a reduced income tax rate of 15%, irrespective of the location of such enterprises in China
- Research and development expenses can be deducted from the taxable income by as much as 150% of the total amount
- More tax incentives will be granted to start-up companies, and enterprises investing in environmental protection, energy and water saving, or industrial safety.
- Existing preferential tax policies for investments in infrastructure facilities, agricultural, forestry, animal husbandry and fishery industries and for those enterprises established in the western regions, have been retained

Existing tax incentives available to those qualifying enterprises which employ laid-off or handicapped workers have been replaced with super deductions applied to the wages paid to disabled employees. For CIT, the super deduction of salary paid to disabled employees is 200%, for IIT, monthly taxes of less than RMB 2000 are exempt.

Three important tax circulars were issued in February 2008 which significantly impact foreign-invested enterprises in China. These circulars further clarified several significant areas of the corporate tax regime including tax incentives for high-technology industries and grandfathering treatments.

Circular Caishui [2008] No. 1, issued 4 February 2008, specifies tax incentives available to certain industries in the tax law. It provides tax incentives to software production companies, IC production companies and security investment funds. These tax incentives mirror the incentives granted under the old tax regime. Preferential tax treatment will also continue to apply to IC production and assembly companies and software production companies newly established in the western region of China. Circular 1 also states that tax holidays for software production companies and IC production companies will start from the first profit-making year.

Grandfathering

Circular 21 clarifies how the half-rate reduction during an unutilized tax holiday period should be calculated during the grandfathering period for qualifying FIEs. Circular 21 states that the half-rate reduction during the unutilized tax holiday period should be calculated based on the gradually increased tax rates of 18, 20, 22 and 24% for the years 2008, 2009, 2010, 2011, respectively, and 25% from 2012 forward. That means the net rates will be 9, 10, 11, 12, and 12.5%, depending on the year in which the half-rate reduction applies. For FIEs that were subject to a 24 or 33% tax rate under the old tax regime, the half-rate reduction during the unutilized tax holiday period should be calculated based on 25%, making the net rate 12.5%.

Old foreign enterprise income tax	Transitional rate (%)	Transition period
15%	18	January 1, 2008
	20	January 1, 2009
	22	January 1, 2010
	24	January 1, 2011
	25	January 1, 2012

Circular Guoshuifa [2008] No. 23, released on 23 February 2008, clarifies aspects of the grandfathering treatments of previously enjoyed tax incentives. To qualify for reinvestment tax refunds, FIEs must have completed all reinvestment steps and obtained the dated business license of the new business license on or before the end of 2007.

For contracts involving interest or royalties that were entered into before 2008, have met the criteria for withholding tax under the old tax regime, and have been already approved by the tax authorities, the withholding tax exemption will continue to apply until the expiration of the original contract. This will not apply to any extension, expansion or supplementary contract of the original contract.

Foreign-invested enterprises eligible for grandfathering treatments of unutilized tax holidays will still need to observe the original requirements stipulated under the old tax law, chief among these would be business scope and operation period. If an FIE fails to fulfill the original requirements, the tax exempted or reduced period during the tax holiday, including the part falling after 2008, would be drawn back.

2 Withholding Tax

Withholding tax is a PRC tax levied on overseas companies providing services to China-based businesses.

For companies based outside of China but who are supplying services to clients in China (this can include a China-based subsidiary), your invoices are in effect "China-derived income" and the Chinese tax authorities levies taxes on these amounts. These are withheld by your client in China, being deducted from your gross invoice amount. This is why many overseas companies without a legal presence in China cannot receive the total gross amount due on their invoices to the China entity.

Your client has the responsibility of passing this tax onto the tax bureau. If they do not, or do not subtract the relevant amount of tax from your invoice, then the

Chinese tax bureau will pursue the local business—and not the overseas operation—for settlement.

The withholding income tax rate is normally 10 percent unless otherwise prescribed in the tax treaty with the relevant foreign government. If the rate in the tax treaty is higher than 10 percent, 10 percent of dividends shall be adopted according to current rules; if the rate in the tax treaty is lower than 10%, the rate in the tax treaty should be adopted.

Tax rate on dividends from tax treaties

Tax rate	Countries (regions)
0%	Georgia (If the beneficial owner holds directly or indirectly at least 50% of the capital of the company paying the dividends and the total investment is no less than EUR2 million)
5%	Kuwait, Mongolia, Mauritius, Slovenia, Jamaica, Yugoslavia, Sudan, Laos, South Africa, Croatia, Macedonia, Seychelles, Barbados, Oman, Bahrain, Saudi Arabia, Ethiopia
5% (Holds directly 10% of the capital of the company paying the dividends)	Venezuela, Georgia (investment in the company paying the dividends is no less than EUR 100,000; 10% of gross dividends if the beneficial owner holds directly less than 10% of the capital of the company paying the dividends)
5% (Holds directly 25% of the capital of the company paying the dividends)	Algeria, Luxemburg, Korea, Ukraine, Armenia, Iceland, Lithuania, Latvia, Estonia, Ireland, Moldova, Cuba, Trinidad and Tobago, Tajikstan, Hong Kong, Macau, Singapore (10% of gross dividends if the beneficial owner holds directly less than 25% of the capital of the company paying the dividends)
7%	United Arab Emirates
7% (Holds directly 25% of the capital of the company paying the dividends)	Austria (10% of gross dividends if the beneficial owner holds directly less than 25% of the capital of the company paying the dividends)
8%	Egypt, Tunisia, Mexico
10%	In all other cases

China has tightened its policies and procedures regarding withholding tax from non-tax resident enterprises for their China-sourced income. Non-resident enterprises with or without establishment or place in China, and those with income not effectively connected with such establishment or place, shall pay CIT on their China-sourced income. Such income includes: income from the sales of goods; income from the provision of services; income from the transfer of property, dividends and profit distribution; income from equity investment, interests, rentals, royalties; income from donation; and any other income not included in the categories listed.

The income tax payable on such income derived by non-resident enterprises shall be withheld at source, and the payer shall be the withholding agent. The withholding agent shall withhold tax from the amount of each payment that is paid or that becomes due at the time of payment or at the time the payment falls due, which means that the withholding obligation arises when such income is remitted or when the payer accrues the amount as a cost or expense under the accrual method of accounting, and the China enterprise who remits the fund overseas shall be the withholding agent. Calculation of tax liability:

$$\text{Withholding tax payable} = \text{taxable income} \times \text{tax rate}$$

For dividends, interest, rental and royalty income, the taxable amount is the gross amount remitted before deduction of any taxes, including business tax. If the withholding tax and business tax is borne by the payer, the amount of income should be grossed up to arrive at taxable income. For dividends paid overseas, no business tax is levied. For income from the transfer of property, the taxable income amount shall be the balance of the total income amount less the net value of the property. For other income, the taxable income amount shall be calculated according to the approaches as mentioned in the preceding two items.

Administration of Withholding Tax

Non-resident enterprises subject to withholding tax in China and the China withholding agents are strongly advised to comply with the procedures to avoid potential penalties. The procedures are applied to a non-resident enterprise's China sourced dividend, interest, rental and royalty income, and income from transfer of property. The filing procedure is fairly straight forward. A copy of the contract giving rise to taxable income, along with a contract registration record for withholding income tax and other relevant documents must be submitted to the in-charge tax bureau within 30 days of signing the contract.

This procedure also applies to each subsequent revision, supplementation or extension of the contract. All documentation, including those originally in a foreign language, must be translated into Chinese. If an equity transfer is between two non-Chinese parties and the transaction takes place outside China, the resident enterprise whose equity is exchanged should file a copy of the share transfer agreement when applying for a change of its tax registration. The seller of the equity should report its taxes on its own or by appointing an agent.

The tax will be withheld from the cash payment by the payer and within 7 days from the payment date, the withholding agent shall pay the amount withheld on each payment to the state treasury and submit the withholding return to local tax authorities. In the case the income is paid by installment, the withholding agent should, within 15 days before making the last payment, report to the tax bureau in charge the details of all payments already paid, together with previous withholding returns and tax payment evidence, to complete a tax withholding clearance.

The China withholding agent should maintain books and records for taxes withheld and a file of the relevant contracts, which will be subject to inspection by tax bureaus.

If the withholding agent fails to fulfill its obligation to withhold tax, non-resident enterprises shall file and pay corporate income tax to the local tax authorities where the income is derived from within 7 days of the due date for tax filing and payment.

3 Value-Added Tax

China's value-added taxes contribute a large percentage of China's annual tax revenue and account for a significant proportion of tax liabilities for many Chinese enterprises. They affect companies that sell, manufacture, process or repair tangible goods in China and can be quite complex.

In China, VAT is administered by the State Administration of Taxation (import VAT is collected by Customs on behalf of SAT), and the tax revenue, except import VAT, is shared between the central government (75%) and local governments (25%). VAT is the major source of fiscal revenue for the government of China, particularly the central government. In 2009, the revenue from VAT amounted to RMB1.84 trillion, accounting for 31% of China's total tax revenue for the year, the largest percentage of the China's annual tax revenues.

China started to implement VAT in 1984 on 24 specified taxable items. On 13 December 1993, the State Council promulgated the *Interim Regulation of the People's Republic of China on Value Added Tax* (VAT Interim Regulations) with the intent of "unifying taxation management, equalizing the tax burden, simplifying the tax system, and guaranteeing financial revenue." This law codified China's VAT system and continued to be in use until November 2008.

In 2004, China introduced VAT reforms in the provinces of Heilongjiang, Jilin and Liaoning in an effort to revitalize the old industrial base of Northeast China. The method of "increment deduction" was adopted and the scope of the reform was confined to eight industries: equipment manufacturing, petrochemical, metallurgy, automobile, shipbuilding, new- and high-tech industries, and agricultural products processing. Following the success of the pilot reform in the Northeast, it was extended in 2007 to 26 old industrial base cities in the Central Chinese provinces of Henan, Hunan, Hubei, Shanxi, Anhui and Jiangxi. In the second half of 2008, five areas of eastern Inner Mongolia and the earthquake-devastated region of Wenchuan in Sichuan Province were also designated as VAT reform pilot areas. In 2009, the central government implemented the VAT reforms nationally.

On November 10, 2008, the State Council of China approved the amendments to the VAT Regulations, which took effect in the beginning of 2009. The key change is a shift from a production-based VAT regime to a consumption-based one. With the exception of specific industries that the state has mandated are to be restricted, all industries in China now fall under the VAT reform system and companies are able to offset the full amount of input VAT paid on newly purchased machinery and equipment against VAT collected when they sell their products.

The main changes to the amended VAT Interim Regulations are as follows:

- Full VAT credit on fixed assets, but VAT-In paid on consumer goods used by taxpayers themselves (for example, cars and yachts) cannot be creditable

- The VAT rate for small scale taxpayers was reduced to 3% from 4 or 6%
- Cancellation of VAT exemption policy on imported equipment for companies in "encouraged" industries
- Cancellation of VAT refund policy on purchasing domestically manufactured equipment for companies in "encouraged" industries
- Cancellation of VAT exemption policy on imported equipment for contract processing, assembly or compensation trade

This is good news for most companies because the measures are expected to reduce the tax burden on companies. However, please be aware that this change could adversely affect cash flow in companies in "encouraged" industries as the aforementioned VAT exemption policies have been abolished. VAT exemptions on imported equipment are now gone and companies will need to increase fund reserves to pay for VAT in advance.

They may also lack sufficient VAT-Out to absorb VAT-In credit (explained in detail below) on fixed assets if they export all or most of their products. The VAT reform also presents an additional tax burden for R&D centers that imported equipment on a tax-free basis in the past. They now have to pay VAT on imported equipment under the new VAT regulation and are not able to claim any credit against their business tax liability. Companies engaged in transfer sales with local customers should note that the VAT-In paid on imported equipment cannot be refunded. In another words, it will be an additional cost under the current VAT system.

Companies may consider setting up new entities in bonded zone to alleviate the impact on cash flow as well as tax burdens arising from the cancellation of preferential VAT exemption on imported equipment imported into bonded zones.

VAT Rates

The Chinese government rules that all enterprises and individuals engaged in the sale of goods, provision of processing, repairs and replacement services, and import of goods within China shall pay VAT. There are a few exemptions, such as self-produced agricultural products sold by agricultural producers, contraceptive medicines and devices, antique books, importation of instruments and equipment directly used in scientific research, experiment and education, importation of materials and equipment from foreign governments and international organizations as assistance free of charge, articles imported directly by the organizations of the disabled for special use by the disabled, and sale of goods which have been used by the sellers. However, pretty much every business will be liable for this tax.

For the sale of goods or taxable services, VAT is incurred on the date when the sales sum is received, or documented evidence of the right to collect the sales sum is obtained. For imported goods, it is incurred on the date of import declaration.

VAT on imported goods is collected by Customs on behalf of the tax authorities. VAT on articles for personal use brought or mailed into China by individuals is levied at the same time as customs duty.

VAT taxpayers are divided into general taxpayers and small-scale taxpayers, and their respective tax obligations are elaborated below.

General Taxpayer Status

According to the *Measures for the Administration of the Qualification Recognition of VAT General Taxpayers* enacted on February 10, 2010, taxpayers with an annual sales value not exceeding the level for small-scale taxpayers set by MOF and SAT as well as taxpayers who have newly established their business may apply to the tax department for recognition as general taxpayers.

However, full general taxpayer status is not instantly granted to wholesalers. Only after passing a 3-month trial testing period as a general taxpayer under a tax officer's supervision can the wholesaler become a fully certified general taxpayer.

VAT Calculation for General Taxpayers

The VAT rate for general taxpayers is generally 17 percent, or 13 percent for some goods (see table below). For taxpayers who deal in goods or provide taxable services with different tax rates, the sale amounts for the different tax rates shall be accounted for separately. If this is not done, the higher tax rate shall apply.

VAT payable relies on two figures: output VAT and input VAT. Output VAT is that payable on the services and goods sold by a company, namely: output VAT = A × B, where A = sales value and B = tax rate. Input VAT is that payable on the goods and services a company buys from another supplier.

The input VAT is used as a credit against the output tax levied on selling the goods. The VAT payable shall be the output VAT for the period, after deducting the input VAT for the period, i.e.:

$$\text{VAT payable} = \text{output VAT} - \text{input VAT}$$

Taxable items	Rate (%)
Exportation of goods (except where otherwise stipulated by the rate)	0
Cereals and edible vegetable oils, tap water, heating, cooling, hot air supplying, hot water, coal gas, liquefied petroleum gas, natural gas, methane gas, coal/charcoal products for household use; books, newspapers, magazines (excluding the newspapers and magazines distributed by the post department); feeds, chemical fertilizers, agricultural chemicals, agricultural machinery and plastic covering film for farming; dressing metal mineral products, agriculture, forestry, products of animal husbandry, aquatic products; audio-visual products; electronic publications; dimethyl ether; edible salt	13
The import and sales of goods other than chose listed above; services of processing, repairs and replacement	17

VAT Calculation for Small Scale Taxpayers

From January 1, 2009, the VAT thresholds for those enterprises that do not qualify for general taxpayer status have been amended. First, the sales threshold for small scale taxpayers has been reduced from RMB 1 million (for enterprises engaged primarily in the production of goods or the provision of taxable services) and RMB 1.8 million (for enterprises engaged in the wholesaling or retailing of goods) to RMB 500,000 and RMB 800,000, respectively. And second, non-enterprise units and entities that normally do not engage in taxable activities are given the choice whether or not they are taxed as small-scale taxpayers while individual (natural person) taxpayers with business turnover exceeding the threshold shall continue to be taxed as small-scale taxpayers. The current VAT rate for small scale taxpayers is 3%.

As such taxpayers cannot deduct input VAT, the formula is as follows:

$$\text{VAT payable} = \text{sales value} \times \text{taxrate (i.e., 3\%)}$$

Export Tax Rebates

Since 1985, China has had in place a tax rebate system designed to support export trade and increase the international competitiveness of companies involved in this business.

Over the past years, Chinese government has been actively discouraging the development of industries which consume high amounts of energy and natural-resources or those that pollute the environment to a great extent by lowering the export refund rates applicable to the relevant products and prohibiting the use of processing trade models.

With China's trade surplus growing rapidly, the central government has made significant changes to its VAT refund system in an attempt to slow export growth. Because of the ongoing changes to the system, export tax rebates and exemptions have now become a major cause for concern among most foreign enterprises.

As the world financial crisis took hold, the central government moved to increase the VAT refund rates on several industries in an effort to boost production. For example, China has increased the tax rebate on textiles at least four times in 2009. In October 2009, the Ministry of Finance raised export tax rebates on 2,486 different types of products, an estimated one-quarter of all exports listed by Chinese customs authorities.

However, there has been a steady recovery in import/exports since 2010. In June 2010, the trend of increasing export rebate rates was reversed when the Ministry of Finance cancelled the export tax rebates for 406 products, mainly high pollution, high energy consumption products.

So exactly who qualifies for export tax rebates? There are two important concepts to understand; the "exemption, deduction and refund" method, and the "maximum refundable amount."

The exemption, deduction and refund method and formula is generally applicable only to production enterprises qualified as general taxpayers (as noted above, there is no refund for small scale taxpayers), which are either directly engaged in export or which consign goods to other import and export enterprises for export.

Exemption, deduction and refund are defined as:

Exemption	goods which are exported by production enterprises either directly or on consignment through foreign trade companies are exempt from VAT-Out.
Deduction	applies to enterprises whose self-produced goods are both exported (directly or through export agents) and sold domestically. The VAT-In credit on materials purchased for the production of export goods is offset against the VAT-Out on domestic sales.
Refund	applies if there is excess input VAT above that amount retained for credit (to be carried forward).

Exemption, deduction and refund calculation:

$$\text{VAT payable} = \text{VAT-Out} - \text{VAT-In} + \text{non-refundable VAT} \\ - \text{VAT-In brought forward from previous period}$$

$$\text{Non-refundable VAT} = (\text{export} - \text{imported free duty raw materials}) \\ \times (\text{levy rate} - \text{refund rate})$$

If VAT payable is a positive figure, then the enterprise will have to pay VAT to the tax bureau, if it is negative, then the tax bureau will refund the enterprise.

Maximum refundable amount calculation:

$$\text{Maximum refundable amount} = (\text{collection amount from overseas for the export sales} \\ - \text{free duty imported raw material}) \times \text{refund rate}$$

If the absolute value of VAT payable is less than the maximum refund amount, the refund amount equals the absolute value of VAT payable. If the absolute value of VAT payable is greater than the maximum refund amount, then the refund amount equals the maximum refund amount (the balance between the absolute value of VAT payable and maximum refund amount will be carried forward to the next period).

Example Assumptions for the example are shown in the following table (in this case, we assume there is no custom duty applied).

Local purchased raw material price	300
Imported raw material price	50
Local sales price	100
Export sales price (assuming the collection has been received in current month)	400
Levy rate	17%
Refund rate	13%

Let us suppose that one-fifth of imported raw material is used for local sales based on the proportion of local sales out of total sales.

The calculation of the refund amount is:

	Calculation	
VAT-Out	100 × 17%	17
VAT-In	300 × 17% + 50 × (1/5) × 17%	52.7
Non-refundable	(400 − 50 × (4/5)) × (17% − 13%)	14.4
VAT payable	(17–52.7) + 14.4	−21.3
Maximum refund amount	(400 − 50 × (4/5)) × 13%	46.8

As the absolute VAT payable is less than the maximum refund amount, the tax bureau will refund RMB 21.3 to the enterprise. Note that no VAT or customs duty is levied on imported raw material used for export sales only if a company uses the Customs Handbook for importing and exporting; for imported raw material used for local sales, VAT and customs duty apply.

Profit and loss for the above case	RMB
Sales	500
Cost of raw material	350
Non-refundable VAT	14.4
Gross margin	135.6

Since the refund rate is different from the levy rate, export-oriented enterprises shall bear additional tax burdens, which ultimately will affect profit and loss.

Export Tax Rebate and Exemption Declaration Procedures

Export enterprises must follow up formal registration of tax refund to apply for a VAT refund or exemption. They should submit the following documentation to the responsible tax authority for the approval of registration, which should be obtained within 30 days from the date of export approval:

- Declaration form
- Business license
- Ministry of Commerce documentation approving export operation

After a production enterprise carries out export procedures and records the sales in their financial statement—based on the requirements of their accounting system—it can apply to the tax bureau for VAT payment and exemption and deduction, and to the same bureau for VAT refunds.

The application period for a tax refund is from the 1st until the 15th of the following month. When an enterprise applies for a VAT payment and exemption or deduction, the following documentation needs to be provided:

- Declaration of VAT payment form and other required forms
- Summary declaration form of VAT exemption, deduction and refund for production enterprise, issued and approved by the local tax refund authority
- Export invoice, import and export declaration form, export proceed cancellation and verification from the State Administration of Foreign Exchange
- Other documents as may be required by the tax authority

For newly incorporated manufacturing companies, accumulated negative VAT payable for the first 12 months cannot be refunded—this amount will be refunded in the 13th month in one lump sum. If the company cannot collect money from overseas customers for the export sales, it also cannot obtain a refund on time. If the company cannot complete the VAT effective date of registration filing for export sales within 90 days (for example: the goods are shipped outside of China and the export declaration form obtained in January, but the VAT effective date of registration filing is not completed prior to the end of March), these export sales must be deemed as the local sales, and are liable for 17% VAT.

4 Business Tax

This is a tax payable against turnover by all enterprises and individuals undertaking the following business: providing taxable services, including communications, transport, construction, finance and insurance, telecoms, culture, entertainment and service industries; transferring the provision of intangible assets; and selling immovable properties.

The basic formula is:

$$\text{Tax payable} = \text{turnover} \times \text{tax rate}$$

Only a very few items are excluded from turnover.

Rates of business tax vary considerably, dependent on industry.

Business tax rates

Industry	Tax rate (%)
Transportation	3
Construction,	3
Finance and insurance	5
Post and telecommunications	3
Culture and sports	3
Entertainment	5–20
Servicing agencies	5
Transfer of intangible assets	5
Sales of immovable properties	5

The Ministry of Finance and State Administration of Taxation jointly issued revised Implementation Rules for Provisional Business Tax Regulations on December 15, 2008, making some fundamental changes to the taxing principals of the business tax regulations. The revised rules took effect on January 1, 2009.

Under the old business tax rules, the service providers were only liable to business tax in China if the taxable service was rendered within China. Thus when a foreign enterprise provided services to China clients and such services were conducted outside China, the foreign enterprise would not be subject to business tax in China. However, under the new rules, the definition of taxable services subject to business tax has been expanded to include services performed where either the service provider or the service recipient is located in China, without regard to where the service is actually been rendered. Therefore, as long as the service provider or service recipient is located in China, the service will be taxable for business tax purposes, regardless of being onshore or off shore. The only exclusion is where both service provider and service recipient are located outside China.

Financial institutions used to be subject to business tax on the trading of foreign exchange, marketable securities and futures, but non-financial institutions and individuals were not. Under the new regime, the trading of foreign currency, marketable securities, non-commodity futures and other financial commodities by any taxpayer are subject to business tax.

Formerly, deemed sales applied only to a company transferring immovable property to other parties without any consideration, however under the new rules, deemed sales apply to either a company or an individual transferring immovable property or land use rights to other companies or individuals without any consideration.

The changes in China's business tax rules have increased the amount of tax paid by multinational service providers with clients in China (see chart below). Service providers should consider modifying billing arrangements with Chinese clients by charging business tax from Chinese clients or arranging for an overseas office to bill and collect payment from their Chinese client's international affiliates if possible.

Before January 1, 2009

Scenario	Service provider	Service recipient	Service provided in China	Service provided outside China	Business taxpayer
A	In China	Outside China	Business taxable	Non-business taxable	In China service provider
B	Outside China	In China	Business taxable	Non-business taxable	Outside China service provider
C	In China	In China	Business taxable	Non-business taxable	In China service provider
D	Outside China	Outside China	Business taxable	Non-business taxable	Outside China service provider

After January 1, 2009

Scenario	Service provider	Service recipient	Service provided onshore China	Service provided offshore China	Business taxpayer
A	In China	Outside China	Business taxable	Business taxable	In China service provider
B	Outside China	In China	Business taxable	Business taxable	Outside China service provider
C	In China	In China	Business taxable	Business taxable	In China service provider
D	Outside China	Outside China	Non-business taxable	Non-business taxable	N/A

Business tax is usually calculated, filed and paid to the local tax bureau every month.

When first registering for business tax, the tax bureau will issue a form showing all the taxes applicable. Businesses must be careful if they are selling goods and services simultaneously, as in these cases there are complicated criteria to judge whether business tax or VAT is applicable. Professional advice is recommended.

5 Consumption Tax

The current consumption tax system was introduced in 1994 along with the nationwide indirect taxes reform, including VAT and business tax.

Consumption tax is levied on five categories of products:

1. Products the overconsumption of which is harmful to health, social order and the environment, e.g., tobacco, alcohol, firecrackers and fireworks
2. Luxury goods and non-necessities, such as precious jewelry and cosmetics
3. High-energy consumption and high-end products, such as passenger cars and motorcycles

4. Non-renewable and non-replaceable petroleum products, such as gasoline and diesel oil
5. Financially significant products such as motor vehicle tires

This tax applies whenever certain luxury or other goods are manufactured, processed or imported. Consumption tax is levied only once. Tax rates vary considerably with the product and the tax paid is computed directly as a cost and cannot be refunded (except in rare cases upon the receipt of a consumption tax special invoice from the domestic supplier for consumption taxes paid for export goods). In addition, consumption tax is part of the base upon which VAT is levied. Be careful if you are processing taxable goods for others, since you are liable to withhold and pay consumption tax based on the value of the raw material and your processing fee. Consumption tax should be filed and paid monthly.

Consumption tax rates

Taxable items	Tax rate	Comments
Tobacco		
Grade A cigarettes	56% or RMB 150 per box (250 cartons)	Includes imported
Grade B cigarettes	36% or RMB 150 per box (250 cartons)	Includes imported
Cigars	36%	
Cut tobacco	30%	
Alcohol		
White spirits	20% plus RMB 0.5 per 500 g/ml	Plus RMB 0.5 per 500 g/ml
Yellow spirits	RMB 240/ton	
Beer	Type A: RMB 250/ton Type B: RMB 220/ton	
Other alcoholic drinks	10%	
Alcohol	5%	
Precious jewelry and precious jade and stones	Gold, silver, platinum and diamond: 5% other precious jewelry and precious jade and stones: 10%	Includes all kinds of gold, silver, jewelry and precious stone ornaments
Firecrackers and fireworks	15%	
Gasoline	Leaded: RMB 1.4/l Unleaded: RMB 1.0/l	
Diesel oil	RMB 0.8/l	
Passenger cars, with a cylinder capacity of		
1.5 l and below	1 l and below: 1% 1–1.5 l: 3%	
1.5–2 l	5%	
2–2.5 l	9%	
2.5–3 l	12%	

(continued)

(continued)

Taxable items	Tax rate	Comments
3–4 l	25%	
Above 4 l	40%	
Small-to-medium size commercial vehicle (e.g. cross country vehicles, minibuses and vans)	5%	
Motorcycles, with a cylinder capacity of		
250 ml below	3%	
Over 250 ml	10%	
Motor vehicle tires	3%	Radial tire exempt
Cosmetics	30%	Luxurious skin-care products are classified as "cosmetics" and are subject to consumption tax at 30%
Golf balls and equipment	10%	
Luxury watches	20%	
Yachts	10%	
Disposable wooden chopsticks	5%	
Solid wood flooring	5%	
Naphtha	RMB 1.0/l	
Solvent oil	RMB 1.0/l	
Lubricating oil	RMB 1.0/l	
Fuel oil	RMB 0.8/l	
Aviation oil	RMB 0.8/l	Temporary exemption

6 Audit

All foreign-invested enterprises in China are required to prepare annual financial statements, including balance sheets and income statements for their annual Chinese audit. Such accounts must be in accordance with the Chinese accounting standards for business enterprises, irregardless of if they are foreign or domestic companies. Foreign-invested enterprises, including their legally responsible persons, must take full responsibility for the truthfulness, legitimacy and completeness of these financial statements. These documents must be completed ahead of the submission of consolidated accounts for tax purposes by the end of April every year, for the financial calendar year ending the previous December 31.

These statements will be used for computing the FIEs taxable and distributable profit. Thus, an annual audit by a firm of certified public accountants registered in the PRC is required under Chinese law.

There are a number of areas where you need to take particular care and where there are some differences between Chinese and western accounting practice. These are guidelines only, as every business is different.

Audit Items often Queried by Chinese Independent Auditors

Adjustments for Foreign Related Payment Income

If the foreign company has paid overseas insurance for their expat employees, it should be noted that this is not tax deductible unless it is recorded as a salary payment with IIT paid. Foreign-sourced income needs to be accounted for by providing evidence of foreign taxes paid with relevant foreign documentation. Otherwise, foreign taxes may be accrued by the FIE.

Related Party Transactions and Transfer Pricing

If your FIE had any transactions with related parties, you must make sure that these were at arm's length and with adequate documentation to substantiate the charges/income, so that the results were not materially affected by related party transactions that were not in the ordinary course of business. Pay particular attention to transfer pricing issues. Tax officials reserve the right to adjust transfer prices, interest charged by related parties based on market prices or even based on the prescribed profit margin. Transfer pricing should not be used as a mechanism to reduce the amount of profit retained in China. The tax bureau regards this as tax evasion and the penalties and repercussions can be severe.

Withholding Obligations

If the FIE made or accrued in its costs or expenses any payments, royalty charges, interest, services or management fees for services performed in China by foreigners (individuals or organizations), pursuant to related contracts and agreement, the relevant withholding obligation should be provided for on an accrual basis. This means 10% withholding enterprise income tax and 5% business tax apply (the tax rate may be different according to individual cases). These charges shall be accompanied by substantial evidence—otherwise they are not deductible. All the above debts in foreign currency also need to be registered with SAFE prior to approval for remittance.

Input VAT

The VAT invoice must be verified by the tax bureau within 90 days of the invoicing date, otherwise it cannot be deducted. Furthermore, if you have any unusual loss of inventory, then the Input VAT related to the inventory previously credited has to be reversed in the period when the loss is recognized.

VAT Refund on Export

For FIEs, VAT refunds on export should be reconciled with the tax bureau. Foreign-invested enterprises should register all export receivables of the previous year with the bureau. Failure to do so may result in the export sales being deemed as domestic transactions, subject to Output VAT if the payment for export sales is not received and related documents are not presented within the deadline.

Stamp Duty

Although not a material issue with much cost, FIEs should not forget to pay stamp duty on all books, records and applicable contracts. Fines for non-compliance outweigh the dutiable value.

7 Profit Repatriation

Your decision on planning for declaration of dividends for repatriation and/or re-investment of profits will obviously depend on the current situation of your Chinese company and its parent company abroad, but there are a number of tax-related factors to bear in mind. This chapter introduces the procedure that must be followed when declaring dividends.

Repatriation of profits may be preferable if your organization requires the funds for re-investment abroad or return to shareholders.

The process for declaring dividends and repatriating funds

1. First of all, the amount of funds available must be confirmed. The final quarter CIT filing for the year in question will be made in early January of the following year, and after this an annual audit must be carried out. The annual clearance process reflects the results of the audit on the accounts, and this is submitted to SAT for approval.
2. Assuming there are no problems with the submitted documents, the State Administration of Taxation will issue a tax receipt confirming the final amount of CIT payable.
3. With this figure defined, the tax payment for the year in question can be completed and the net profit figure derived.
4. Not all profit can be repatriated or reinvested. A portion of the profit (which must be at least 10% for WFOEs) must be placed in a reserve fund account. This is treated as part of owner's equity on the balance sheet. This account is capped when the amount of reserves equals 50% of the registered capital of the company. In addition the investor may choose to allocate some of the remainder to a staff bonus or welfare fund or an expansion fund, although these are not mandatory for WFOEs.

5. The remaining balance is available for redistribution. Firstly, a resolution of the board of directors to authorize such redistribution must be signed by each director. Then an application form supported by the following documents must be submitted to the SAT:

- Annual audit
- Capital verification report
- Annual clearance report
- Quarterly CIT filings
- Receipts proving CIT payments have been made in full
- Bank and general details of the Chinese entity and entities receiving funds

6. SAT will review all these documents to check that everything is legitimate and issue an evidence of CIT payment certificate.
7. This certificate authorizes the bank to disperse funds as detailed on the certificate.

Note that dividends from profits made after January 1, 2008 are subject to a 10% withholding tax while those dividends connected to profits made prior to January 1, 2008 are exempt from this withholding tax. A lower withholding rate may be applicable under double tax treaties.

Glossary of Terms

AIC	Administration of Industry and Commerce
BOFTEC	Bureau of Foreign Trade and Economic Co-operation (local approvals authority)
CIT	Corporate Income Tax
CJV	Co-operative Joint Venture
EPZ	Export Processing Zone (state level)
EJV	Equity Joint Venture
ETDZ	Economic and Technological Development Zone (state level)
FDI	Foreign Direct Investment
FICE	Foreign Invested Commercial Enterprise
FIE	Foreign Invested Enterprise
FTZ	Free Trade Zone (state level)
HIDZ	Hi-Tech Industrial Development Zone (state level)
IIT	Individual Income Tax
JV	Joint Venture
LLJG	lai liao jia gong (a contract manufacturing/processing agreement, common in South China)
M&A	Merger and Acquisition
MOFCOM	Ministry of Commerce
MOF	Ministry of Finance
NDRC	National Development and Reform Commission

PRC	People's Republic of China
RMB	Renminbi (Chinese currency unit, also know as Yuan or, colloquially, "kuai")
RO	Representative Office
SAFE	State Administration of Foreign Exchange
SAIC	State Administration of Industry and Commerce
SAT	State Administration of Taxation
SDPC	State Development and Planning Commission
SETC	State Economic and Trade Commission
SEZ	Special Economic Zone (state level)
VAT	Value Added Tax
WFOE	Wholly Foreign Owned Enterprise (known colloquially as Woofies")
WTO	World Trade Organisation

ASIA BRIEFING
Regional Business Intelligence
From the Asia Foreign Direct Investment Practice Dezan Shira & Associates
CHINA BRIEFING
www.china-briefing.com
INDIA BRIEFING
www.india-briefing.com
2point6billion.com
www.2point6billion.com
VIETNAM BRIEFING
www.vietnam-briefing.com
RUSSIA BRIEFING
www.russia-briefing.com
www.asiabriefingmedia.com

The manufacturer's authorised representative in the EU is Springer Nature Customer Service Centre GmbH, Europaplatz 3, 69115 Heidelberg, Germany. If you have any concerns regarding our products, please contact ProductSafety@springernature.com

Printed and bound by CPI Group (UK) Ltd, Croydon, CR0 4YY

30/09/2026

02225664-0006